UNDER
THE WIGS

UNDER THE WIGS

Sydney Aylett

EYRE METHUEN LONDON

First published in 1978
by Eyre Methuen Ltd
11 New Fetter Lane, London EC4P 4EE
Copyright © 1978 Sydney Aylett
and Leigh Crutchley

Printed in Great Britain by
Hazell, Watson & Viney Ltd., Aylesbury, Bucks

ISBN 0 413 38690 2

To Leigh (Reggie) Crutchley
Who made the journey

List of Illustrations

Acknowledgements and thanks are due to His Honour Judge Leonard for Plate no. 5; to Radio Times Hulton Library for Plate nos. 3, 4 a and 4 b; to Universal Pictorial Press for Plate nos. 7 a and c; to Keystone Press Agency for Plate no. 7 b; to Barratts Photo Press Ltd for Plate no. 8 a; to Mr Justice Maurice Drake for Plate no. 8 b; and to Butterworth & Co. and the heirs of Theo Mathew for permission to reproduce the cartoons in Plate 6 from *Fifty Forensic Fables* by O (1949).

Preface

Knowing the exactness of lawyers' minds, knowing that lawyers are as sensitive to criticism as other mortals, and knowing that they have at their finger tips the power to seek retribution, this has not been as easy a book to write as I had first thought. I became quickly aware that I was walking a greasy pole. I might well have abandoned the idea if I had not also known that lawyers are a loyal, generous and understanding lot with an acute sense of fun and that therefore they would bear with an old man whose memory for detail and dates has grown dimmer over recent years and who may, despite his past acquaintance with the Law, have strayed over the permissible boundaries in some of his comments.

Let me declare that I bear malice towards none. Indeed, as I have written my account I have realised how much I owe to my many friends at the Bar, and how full and enriched my life has been through knowing them. This they have demonstrated by their willingness not only to refresh but to correct my memory. In particular I must mention Lord Diplock, Mr Justice Drake, Judge Leonard and Lord Hailsham. I also earlier received great encouragement and assistance from Edward Grayson and Gordon Corner, and enthusiastic support throughout from my wife Dora, my daughter Carol Ann and my son-in-law Terry Gill. Then there was Jenny Boreham who not only did the typing but made many helpful suggestions, and finally Leigh (Reggie) Crutchley to whom I dedicate this book and but for whom it might never have been written.

Prologue

The date was 25 July 1973. The place was Lincoln's Inn. The occasion was a dinner to pay tribute to my fifty-eight years as a barristers' clerk in the Temple.

It was later described as, 'A unique and historic event', but it didn't feel like it at the time. To me, it was a gathering of friends. At seventy-two years of age I was the oldest present; even the next in seniority had at one time been one of my 'boys', either as a pupil in chambers, or a young barrister, and though there was in attendance a Lord Chancellor, a Lord of Appeal and several other members of the judiciary, as well as a sprinkling of Queen's Counsel and many barristers, I was not overawed. I felt like a nurse, who although her charges have grown up, still thinks of them as babies.

While we were taking our drinks in the Great Hall, I was reminded of the words of Charles Lamb, whose father, like me, had been a barristers' clerk, and of whom he had written, 'He was at once his clerk, his good servant, his dresser, his friend, his "flapper", his guide, stop watch, auditor, treasurer'. I could add to this list. Since Lamb had written the position of the clerk had increased. As the guests arrived I found myself regarding them as puppets which I, as their maker, had manipulated. Their movements and actions had been my life's work. I had pulled the strings. It was a conceit that no one present would have denied me.

We moved for dinner into the Bencher's drawing-room. It was now that the sense of occasion took hold of me, through the surroundings rather than the people. It was a splendid room, and as I looked round the portraits on the wall I saw that Sir Thomas More, a former Bencher, was gazing down on the assembled company. His presence was a sharp reminder of the man I missed most from this gathering, Theobald Mathew, for More had been his 'angel'. Although Theo had died before the war, his spirit had not died with him, for at least three people present had been his pupils, and one of these, the Lord Chancellor, Lord Hailsham, had, I remembered, written a poem about him under the title of 'Legal Ghosts'.

And last of these, dear Theo, you
Well earned rest of length have sought
Wittiest of spectres who
Haunt the leafy Inns of Court.

Hands clasped backwards, tilted hat,
Humming voice, abstracted pose
Pince-nez spectacles that set
Halfway down the lifted nose.

Master-pleader, plead once more
For your leafy Inns of Court
That peace returning may restore
The havoc lawless hands have wrought.

Theo Mathew it was who had given my life quality. It was through meeting and working with him that I first came to touch greatness and goodness. I later had some similar experiences, but first love it is that retains its lasting sweetness.

My thoughts jolted back to the present. I remembered that dinner over, I would have to respond to a toast. Again, this had no fears for me. I had only a few carefully chosen words to say. Nobody but a fool would, in my position, have considered attempting a speech in company with men whose powers of oratory were so much part of their livelihood.

The evening followed its prescribed course. A presentation was made, many compliments were paid me, and I was eventually hard put to it to stem the tears. Finally the goodbyes were being said. With them came the inevitable question, 'What are you going to do with yourself now, Sydney?' I had no plans. For want of anything to say, I answered, 'Write a book, I suppose.' My remark was received with laughter, but later the more I thought about it, the more I felt it to be the only thing to do for an old man with little left but his memories. So I began.

Chapter One

It was of course a foregone conclusion that I should leave school at fourteen. Most children of lower-middle class families did regardless of any academic ability they might have had, and I was by no means a dunce or dullard. Moreover, I had inherited a shrewdness from my parents, which was further developed by my association with the boys of St John's School, Fulham, which I attended daily for seven years.

As my fourteenth birthday drew near I had no idea what I wanted to do or be, which was probably just as well since at that time it was something that was decided by parents; children who had ideas, and were bold enough to declare them, came into conflict with mothers and fathers, which generally only ended very painfully. In our family only one person made important decisions, and that was my mother. She did go through the motions of involving my father and myself one evening, early in 1915. She had cleared away the supper things and, noticing my father making the signs of a man about to go out for a drink, she announced, 'You can sit down again, Albert, you're not going to the pub yet. We've got to decide, here and now, about our Sydney's future. He'll be leaving school in a few weeks, and it's high time we started looking around for a job for him. Fond though I am of the boy', and she gave me an approving glance, 'I don't want him at home under my feet for too long, and as you well know, Bert', and she gave Pop a meaningful nod, 'the devil finds work for idle hands. Now what are your views on the subject?' Pop removed the pipe from his mouth, scratched his head and said, 'Well er,' then he stopped. Mum didn't give him another chance to comment. 'As I expected,' she waded in, 'you haven't given the matter a thought, so it's just as well that I have. In fact I've more than thought, I've done something about it.' I saw Pop's face brighten. He'd had the sharp end of Mum's tongue, now he knew he was off the hook, he'd only got to listen and then agree to whatever she'd decided. I too was glad that the exchange between them was over; I wanted to hear what lay ahead for me.

'Now I think we're all agreed,' resumed Mum, 'that we want to do our best for Sydney. He's done pretty well at school and we must build on that. His health isn't strong enough for him to go into trade, his reading and writing's good, so it's my considered opinion he should go in for clerking.' She paused for a moment, not because she expected any agreement or disagreement, but to let her words sink in. 'I know it's a funny thing to say,' she went on, 'but it seems the war is on our side. A lot of young men are either enlisting or being called up, so there are quite a few vacancies around. Mrs Francis' husband was saying that there's a job going in his department at the War Office, so I've written there on Sydney's behalf; I've also heard that they want a junior in some chambers in the Temple, so I've applied there too.' 'What Temple, where?' Pop's curiosity got the better of his tongue – he told me some time later he'd had visions of me indulging in Babylonian delights. 'It's a place in the City, where all the lawyers work,' said Mum tartly, as though amazed at his ignorance, though I was sure she had had to have it explained to her. 'So it's war or law, Sydney,' Pop quipped, 'which do you prefer?' Not knowing what either job entailed, I chose war; it seemed more topical and more romantic. 'He hasn't been offered either yet.' Mum's words brought us back to earth. 'Still, as I said, it looks as though there are plenty of opportunities around, but it's as well someone's doing something about them. All right Albert, you can go out now, and Sydney, you can help with the washing up.'

In the event it was law not war that won my services. The vacancy at the War Office had been filled, but soon Mr Packer, chief clerk to Harold Simmons, principal of a set of chambers at

Number 4, Elm Court at the Inner Temple, invited Mum and me to attend for interview at ten o'clock the following Monday morning. Mum moved fast, and that Monday saw me fitted out in what I suppose would be described as a discreet suit, with mackintosh neatly folded over my left arm and a shining black bowler squarely planted on a well-greased head. Mum was also dressed up for the occasion. I couldn't help wondering why she had laid it on so thick, after all it was me that was going after the job, still I felt no end of a dog as we walked to Parson's Green Station. It seemed that everyone was looking at us, but with the security of Mum by my side, and with her, 'They're ignorant, Sydney, take no notice,' I was able to ignore the guffaws and coarse remarks that were directed at us. We travelled direct to Temple Station, where Mum consulted some directions she'd written down, and we set off down the Embankment towards Blackfriars. It was now that Mum's notes ran out. Fortunately there was a road sweeper nearby, who directed us into Inner Temple Gardens, and there we found Elm Court facing the gardens. I always remembered that sweeper, and in my more opulent days I dropped him a penny or two whenever we met.

Harold Simmons' set of rooms was on the ground floor. There was no question of us making a mistake about this, as his name and those of the other barristers in his chambers were painted outside on the wall near the front door. There was another set above, headed by the name F. E. Smith. It meant nothing to me at the time, but I soon learned that I was working close to a man who was one of the great advocates of the day, and later, as Lord Birkenhead, was to become Lord Chancellor. Mum knocked on Simmons' door and it was opened by a man of about twenty-eight, who introduced himself as Mr Packer, chief clerk. Although to me at that time anyone in their twenties was oldish he was much younger than I had expected, and somehow youth seemed out of place in these surroundings. He was sprightly with it, and I could see the surprise on his face as he looked at my mother, a surprise that was mingled with pleasure. As I learned later, women were seldom seen in the Temple, and an attractive one was a rarity. He was all attention as he ushered us along the corridor

3

and into his tiny box-room of an office. A chair appeared from somewhere for Mum, while he and I remained standing.

For the first five minutes Mum and he chattered away. He asked where we lived; when Mum told him he said, 'Oh, I've played cricket near there.' 'You're fond of cricket, are you? It's a most interesting game,' Mum said. 'You enjoy watching it?' 'Oh very much indeed. Unfortunately I don't get so much time nowadays, but when I was a young girl in Leicester' – 'Oh I've seen Surrey play them at the Oval,' and so it went on, with her showing a knowledge of the game that I never dreamed she had. I had always thought that she looked on it as a waste of time. From there they went on to the war, with Mr Packer bemoaning the fact that he was unfit for service – 'Stomach trouble'. That I knew to be one of Mum's favourite subjects, so I shifted my weight on to my other foot and held the desk in front of me, feeling more and more of a spare part.

I don't know whether it was the animated conversation that started it off, but first the far door of the corridor opened, footsteps approached, a figure in a black jacket and striped trousers glanced in as he passed by the door to what, from the sound of an emptying cistern, I later guessed to be the lavatory. On the return journey he paused at our door, then with a slight bow of the head and a 'Good morning', he went on his way. There was a minute's pause with Mum's and Mr Packer's conversation droning on to the accompaniment of the cistern refilling, then a nearer door opened and a similar procedure followed. I think this must have jolted Mr Packer away from his ailments, since his attention now became focused on me, my qualifications and the job, for by the time the third and nearest door opened, and the lavatory was put to further use, they were well into the business of my suitability for a career in the Law. 'He seems rather small for his age,' said Packer.

'He is,' agreed Mum, 'but good stuff in little room.' 'Can he write well, clearly and distinctly?' 'Yes, all three.' 'Does he really want to come into the Law?' 'He's been keen on it for the last three years, haven't you Sydney?'

At last I was brought into the conversation, probably because Mum needed me to support what she knew to be a downright lie. 'Yes Sir, it has always fascinated me,' I said glibly. Mr Packer turned and looked hard at me. 'There's one thing you'll have to do if you wish to succeed. You must go to night school and learn shorthand and typing, for although you will find there are many chambers without a typewriting machine, and many barristers and solicitors that dislike them, I consider the time is shortly coming when they will be universally adopted, and anyone skilled in their use will rise to the top.' Again Mum promised, on my behalf, that I would attend night school regularly. 'He's a quick learner and it won't be long, I promise you Mr Packer, before he has mastered both.'

'Now there's the question of money.' Mr Packer paused, and Mum smiled at him. 'The last junior got five shillings a week,' he continued. Mum's smile, I thought, became a little more appealing. Mr Packer couldn't resist it. 'We'll make it seven shillings then.'

'That will do splendidly,' said Mum. Mr Packer turned to me once more. 'Then you can consider yourself engaged, Billy.' 'Billy!' He had forgotten my name already and my expression must have shown my thoughts, for he burst out laughing, 'Oh, I forgot to tell you, junior clerks in these particular chambers are called Billy, it's part of the terms of employment. You've no objections have you?'

'No, of course he doesn't mind,' Mum said. 'Now when can he start? No time like the present, eh Sydney?' Here Mum gave me the option. 'I'd like that,' I replied. 'You'll need some money for your lunch and your fare.' Mum opened her bag and handed me a shilling. 'Well I'll be off then, thank you very much Mr Packer, and good morning.' Mr Packer wasn't letting her go as easily as that. He escorted her from the office and described the best way to Temple Station. 'You're a lucky boy to have such a charming mother,' he said when he returned, beaming and rubbing his hands. 'Now I expect it's all been a bit of an ordeal for you, and since I have some urgent matters to attend to you can take half an hour off, have a cup of coffee and when you come back I will introduce you to your principals, and then try and initiate you into the mysteries of the Law.'

Mr Packer directed me to a coffee shop in Fleet Street. 'It's opposite the Royal Courts of Justice, where much of our work sees the light of day,' he added. I ran off to celebrate my election to what I considered to be man's estate. Any boy's first job at that time was a milestone in his life, it lifted him away from his fellows and mine was surely no ordinary job, my surroundings showed that. There was a stateliness and solemnity about them that I felt must make me superior to the ordinary type of city clerk. That priggish thought stopped me in my tracks; I must not run here, my bearing must reflect the dignity of the place and my position. I took a deep breath, straightened my shoulders and, discarding childish things, proceeded at what I thought was a proper pace to the coffee shop. At first I found the spirited chatter of those around me disconcerting, it made me feel more alone, but then I began to wonder what it was about my life that had destined me for a career in the Law?

I had been born in Leicester, on 25 January 1901, three days after Queen Victoria's death. My father, Albert Charles Gilbert Aylett, was an electrician employed by the Leicester Corporation. My mother, whose maiden name was Lucy Mallet, was one of four sisters and two brothers. She lived at home until she was married, where she learned how to cook and to keep house. I was four when my sister Elsie was born, thus completing our family. I have been told that I looked a very bonny baby, chubby and rosy, for my mother believed in keeping me in the open air; unfortunately she didn't see to it that my face was shielded from the sun, and as a result my eyes were weakened, and never recovered, so that I have always been short-sighted – that, at any rate, was the diagnosis at the time, and no one since has given any other reason. I was also breast-fed for nine months, and when I went on to cow's milk, I caught some bug which did my stomach no good, so I became what was then called a sickly child, and was cosseted and given all the love, care and attention that were lavished on delicate children by mothers who stayed at home. It wasn't until I was seven years old that I was allowed to go to school, which was all very nice at the time, but eventually created a hurdle which took some getting over. Perhaps it was this early ill-health that affected my growth and height, for I've never stood more than five feet five in my stockinged feet, and slim with it.

The earliest smell that I can remember was that of grease paint, for my father's heart was in the theatre, or perhaps I should be more exact and say the music hall. Any night that he could escape from the house, he would spend at Leicester's Royal or Palace Theatres, often seeing the show through twice at no extra expense, for he was a friend of the managers. On any pretext he would make his way back stage, and if possible into the dressing-rooms. Despite what Mum said, this wasn't time wasted, for he was an excellent mimic, and whenever a particular artist took his fancy, he'd sit in the theatre, write down the act, and, after re-hearsing it at home, would add it to the repertoire of items that he performed at concerts and gigs, in and around Leicester. Eugene Stratton was his favourite, indeed Pop became known as the Eugene Stratton of the Midlands. I believe he made quite a bit of money from these appearances, but this was small consolation for Mum who said that most of it found its way down his throat. As I got a bit older he would often take me with him to the theatre, to the first house. 'Where's my chaperone?' he would say, then adding with a wink, 'Your mother reckons that with you in my arms, I'll have my hands full, and there'll be no room left for a chorus girl.' I don't think there ever was either. He liked the halls for their own sake. Mum knew this and despite her constant digs, there was always a sense of underlying affection in their relation-ship.

I was never able to find out exactly why we left Leicester and in 1908 went to London. However, one day it was announced that Pop had rented a shop in Brewer Street, in the West End, had taken a partner and that together they were going to run an electrical business. I don't know whether he expected to find that the streets were paved with gold, or if he knew that Soho was near theatreland, with the delights of the Palladium, the Colos-seum, the Holborn Empire, the Alhambra and many other houses all within walking distance. Anyway at the time I wasn't concerned with the reason; for me it was a great adventure. I'd never been to London, but from what I'd heard about it, it did spell magic to me.

I was of course disappointed in what I found; for three months while we were looking for a house, we stayed with Pop's brother in cramped quarters in Lewisham. It was a nice respectable suburb, but it was dull compared with our life in Leicester, and two or three visits to the West End didn't compensate. Eventually Mum found a house to rent in Fulham, 78 Chesilton Road. Now Fulham may not have been a fashionable address at the time, but it was near the centre of town and not far from the Bohemian Chelsea where Pop said the artists, writers and free thinkers all lived. Later my chums and I would wander around there, occasionally chiiking the long-haired men with flowing cloaks that we saw in the High Street. We found that though they may have been peculiar-looking they could move fast, and aim as good a kick or cuff as any ordinary mortal; so we learned to live and let live. Pop introduced me to the music halls of the district; the Granville, Walham Green was the nearest, but the better-class houses were the Chelsea Palace and the Hammersmith Palace.

78 Chesilton Road was a large house for a family of four, but Mum had plans for it. She was uncertain how the electrical business would succeed, and so she decided to let two of the rooms to lodgers. Her enterprise prospered, largely as a result of her splendid cooking. She made arrangements with neighbours who had spare rooms so that they supplied accommodation, while she provided the meals. Apart from the extra money it brought in, it gave her the independence she wanted. She was a great supporter of women's rights and was a member of the suffragette movement. I knew Pop disapproved of it, most men did at that time, he used to joke about it outside with his friends, but I never heard him voice a word of criticism in the house. I think in a grudging sort of way it was another thing that made him proud of her. I had cause to be grateful for her culinary success. I was now attending St John's, a nearby Church school, and because of my late start was way behind the other children. But rumours of Mum's meals reached the ears of the head of the Junior School, Miss Webb, and she and another senior teacher, Miss Grace, asked Mum if she could provide lunches for them. She jumped at the idea. The three of them saw eye to eye about

women's rights and got on splendidly. So when Mum explained the reason for my backwardness, I was given individual tuition, and I quickly made up the ground I had lost. Their friendliness also helped my relationship with the other children, for with my poor eyesight and comparative ill-health, I might well have been the target for their ridicule and hostility; as it was, I was regarded as a sort of protected area and I think that this, and my quick wit, made it possible for me to keep pace with my fellows. Another thing that helped me gain their respect was a Sunday School concert. As St John's was a Church school, most of the children met again on Sunday afternoon. I thought it strange that Mum allowed me to go because she was a Pentecostal, a religious group with very high moral standards, but I expect she thought it best for everyone if I conformed.

About twice a year, for the benefit of parents and friends, a concert was presented in the church hall. The programme generally consisted of groups or individuals singing sacred numbers, reciting religious poems, or ballads on the evils of drink. It was with some trepidation, therefore, that when I was asked if I could do anything I agreed, and then did an imitation of Pop doing an imitation of Eugene Stratton. It went down like a bomb with my classmates, though I could see from the expression on the faces of the teachers that they were more than a little un-certain of its suitability. 'That was very nice, Sydney, but don't you know anything a little more in keeping with the occasion?' one of them said. Only knowing a few that were less in keeping, I shook my head. The class, however, took up my cause, and eventually it was agreed that I should be allowed to perform, 'somewhere near the end perhaps,' the teacher said. In the event I came last; I didn't tell them that at the Halls it was the place reserved for whoever was topping the bill. Following the kind of material that had gone before, I'd have had to have given a dismal performance not to have set the house alight. I hadn't much of a singing voice but I knew how to put a number across, and with due modesty I can say that I was the success of the afternoon. At school it gained me a respect in my own right. Even Mum was impressed, and when Pop remarked that I was a chip off the old block, she let it go without comment.

When I went into the Senior School it was discovered that I had another talent, the ability to sketch. I used to practise at home in the winter evenings. Copies of *Punch* occasionally found their way from the lodgers' rooms into our living-room, and I began by copying some of the pen and ink drawings. One day, at the beginning of our art lesson, the teacher told us that we could draw whatever we liked, so I dashed off a few of the sketches that I could remember, and then greatly daring caricatured a few members of the staff. The master was delighted. The following day I was asked to go and see the headmaster. He had my drawings in front of him and he too was very complimentary as he glanced through them. 'This is excellent work, Aylett, you must do some more of these. They are the sort of thing I like to keep to show the Board of Education Inspectors when they visit us.' When he came to the sketches of the staff he smiled slightly. 'Mmm,' he murmured, 'very interesting, but I don't think we'll let out imagination run away with us too much, do you?' I of course agreed, and confined my work to copying from *Punch*.

Although my school days were uneventful, I was never bored. There was always something to look forward to, even if often the anticipation proved greater than the realisation. At weekends I went around with four or five other boys, in a sort of gang. The streets were our playground and though occasionally we got into mischief, we were never destructive or malicious; perhaps it was fear, fear of getting caught, fear of the police, and the greater fear of our parents finding out. Yet I wasn't afraid of my parents. I looked on Pop as a friend, almost as one of us boys, for he occasionally flouted authority, Mum's authority that is, and his knowing that I shared his secret kept us close. I think I held my mother in awe. I respected her and loved her, but she seemed at that time almost superhuman, incapable of doing anything wrong, more a figure to worship.

The First World War, as we now call it, was declared in the August before my last term at school. While it came as a surprise, it didn't upset life much, at any rate at the beginning. Like everyone else my family and friends all thought it would be over by Christmas. The only change it made, as far as I was concerned, was that instead of playing Cowboys and Indians, we changed to British and Germans, with nobody wanting to be the Germans. Patriotic songs took over at the music halls and the Kaiser became a figure of ridicule. Some of the boys' fathers joined up but Pop was too old, so our home life was unaffected. Although I was enjoying school, I was looking forward to leaving, but as I have said, I was quite content to leave my future in my parents' hands. I suppose if I had had any choice I would have liked to have gone into the theatre in any capacity, but if the thought ever entered my mind, it quickly left it. While Pop might have encouraged me, and even tried to help, Mum would never have agreed. She looked on it as some kind of ogre; it was always her feeling that if Pop hadn't squandered his time around the halls he'd have been a lot more successful in his business. All of which, in retrospect, is probably true, but he enjoyed his life as near to the full as he could, and was certainly a nicer person for it.

'Are you going to sit here all day over one cup of coffee?' I was jolted back from my daydreaming by a waitress standing over me with a bill in her hand. I quickly glanced at my watch and saw that my half-hour break was nearly up. I stood, took the bill and mumbling my apologies made my way to the cashier. As I returned through the Temple I remembered what Pop had told me about it. He'd done some research among his friends since our earlier talk with Mum. 'It's where the actors prepare their lines for the greatest dramas of all,' he said impressively. I suppose he was right. I wondered what my part would be. Never more than a very small one I accepted philosophically.

Chapter Two

On my return to 2 Elm Court I sensed that I had in some way incurred Mr Packer's displeasure. He was sitting at his desk busily writing, and he kept me standing there for several seconds before raising a stern face. 'Billy,' he said severely, 'while I realise that you have only been in the Temple for a very short time, I would have thought that the surroundings indicated to anyone with the smallest intelligence that haste within their precincts is unbecoming, and also that all those concerned with the Law, even the most lowly, dress in a seemly fashion. Not only were you seen running from the Temple, but you failed to wear a hat.' I mumbled my apologies. 'Even the messengers, with their urgent communications, never break into a trot, and they are always correctly dressed,' he went on. He meant to make his point, and to establish his authority from the beginning. He was of course referring to the messengers who were still used for special deliveries to and from the solicitors' offices in the city. I later found out that some three or four years previously it had been common practice to use our own messengers almost entirely. They were employed by the Temple, and sat about on benches waiting to be summoned. Even though the post was more reliable then than it is now and much cheaper, old customs died hard.

Although there was a telephone installed in our chambers, it was mistrusted as a form of communication; appointments would occasionally be made through it but it was many years before matters were discussed on it. Theobald Mathew, whom I later worked for, actively detested the thing and, if he was ever called to speak on it, made his feeling known to whoever was on the other end of the line. When I first saw the telephone directory for the whole of the London area, it was scarcely an inch thick. The only thing that lawyers believed in was the written word, and I mean hand-written, solicitors mistrusted Pleadings or Opinions that were typed, and it was a long time before the 'mechanical word' became generally accepted. Few sets of chambers possessed typewriters; we had one, though it needed attention; the 'e' key stuck every time it was struck and despite the fact that I drew it to Mr Packer's notice several times, since I was using it to practise on, it was not repaired whilst I was there.

Having put me firmly in my place, Mr Packer decided that I was now ready to be shown to those for whom I was to work. I was first taken to a large room at the end of the corridor, to meet the head of chambers, Mr Harold Simmons. After Mr Packer had introduced me, he looked me up and down and said, 'So you're our new Billy, are you? I bid you welcome, and I hope you will be with us for a very long time. We don't like change around here do we Packer, eh?' Then he asked me a few questions about my schooling. 'Well, work hard, my boy, and you'll get on famously.' Just as we were leaving he said, 'I take it that lady you were with was your mother, Billy; dashed attractive women, eh Packer?' Mr Packer agreed, and ushered me out of the room. 'A genial cove', was my immediate reaction to him; it was one that stuck with me until I left. The next room was shared by a Mr Lewis Moses and a Mr Maxwell Thin. Mr Moses was out. Mr Thin I discovered had recently left the army and was trying to rake up a practice. I didn't see a lot of him for at that time he was not having much success. He couldn't find a lot to ask me or to say to me, but, like Mr Simmons, as I left he complimented me on my mother.

In the third and smallest room I met Colin Duncan. At first I thought with a name like that he must be a Scot but he was in fact Irish, and with all the charm of his birthplace. He too was struggling at that time, but he later became a skilful protagonist, whose advice and services were much in demand. Again after a few smiling words of welcome, he heralded my exit with a reference to my mother's charms, so that when we landed back in Mr Packer's room and he asked me what I thought of my lords and masters I couldn't resist replying that it was my opinion they considered my mother should have been given the job. I expected a rebuke for my cheekiness, but he seemed to think it no end of a joke for he slapped me on the back and said, 'You and I are going to get on like a house on fire, Billy, I like a sense of humour. People think the law is as dry as dust, but it's like any other job, there's a deal of fun in it if you know where to look.'

Packer now began my initiation. He didn't mince his words, he told me I had joined what was a poor set of chambers. He explained that Mr Simmons had only recently been called to the Bar, that before that he had been a solicitor with the Jewish firm Steadman, Van Prague and Gaylor, and that he'd seen his opportunity to change horses when the Money Lenders Act was passed. This Act had hit the money lenders hard, as it gave borrowers a loophole to escape from their contract if it was found that the terms were harsh and unconscionable, meaning unreasonable, and since the majority of lenders were Jews, they rushed to their solicitors to find out how this was likely to be interpreted in Law. As there were few if any barristers at that time to give opinions, Harold Simmons had stepped into the breach. He was an opportunist, and it was the springboard he needed to become a successful barrister. Douglas Hogg, later to become the first Lord Hailsham, was another expert in this side of the law, though according to Mr Simmons Hogg liked to take a look at his own Pleadings because he knew he was the best man at the job. It may have been vanity on Simmons' part. I was to find out there was plenty of that in the Temple.

Packer then moved to the structure of our legal system. He began with solicitors, to whom we were beholden for our work. He didn't seem to care for them very much; according to him some weren't so bad as others. Later he tempered this a little when he said, 'Remember, Billy, when you meet them, or their clerks, not to show any ill feelings you may have towards them. They are our bread and butter, you'll soon learn to sort the sheep from the goats and when you get into a good set of chambers, then's the

14

time that you'll be able to make it known who's the boss and who it is who makes the decisions.' Solicitors were the link between the client and the barrister; they advised clients and instructed and prepared causes, that is the matter or reason about which a person goes to law, while the Pleadings or law suits were the arguments put forward by the barristers in court, either for or against a case.

As Packer explained in more detail the position of the barristers it did not make sense to me. I could accept that they were not allowed to advertise, I knew that doctors could not. But when I was told that barristers could not approach solicitors directly, that they could not fix a fee for their services, this again being done by the clerks, and that if either the client or the solicitor did not pay, they could not sue for their money, that their fees were considered to be an honorarium, and finally that when they were given briefs and appeared in court, it was generally months, and sometimes years before they were paid by solicitors, I wondered how anyone could be so foolish as to contemplate the profession. In addition I learned that in return for all these 'thou shalt nots' there was the probability that in their first five years at the Bar, their earnings would be no more than would pay for a few hot dinners. Yet according to Packer the chambers and the Temple were full, and there were plenty of young men knocking at the door.

Packer must have sensed my astonishment for he went on to say that once a barrister began to make a name for himself, the eventual reward could be very high indeed. Then he added, 'That's where I come in, Billy, and where I hope you will some day. You see my boy, to a great degree the money that I earn relates to what they earn. I get, as it were, a percentage of their pay; I will explain to you later how this works because until you have some understanding of what it is we do, you won't have any idea of what I am talking about.' 'You mean you don't get a fixed salary?' I queried. 'No, that's not quite true, I couldn't manage without a living wage, the money takes too long to come in. I receive an amount guaranteed me by Mr Simmons, who gets a share of this from each of the members in the chambers, but if the percentage due to me exceeds it, then I have the difference between the two amounts in addition to my weekly stipend.' 'So it's as though you're on a commission?' 'You could say that, though I prefer to look on myself as a kind of theatrical agent, who takes a percentage of what his artists earn, because just as an agent gets his performers work, in the same way I, and those like me in other chambers, do the same. However, don't you run away with the idea that I earn a lot of money, I don't, but I mean to. This, as I've said, is not a good set of chambers; at the moment we get too much poor work, that is work we don't get paid for, which a young barrister may be pleased to do for the sake of experience, but which is no use to me. However things are looking up and once you get the hang of things here, I intend that they will improve by leaps and bounds.'

I couldn't see how my presence was going to make that kind of difference, and I said so. Packer was patient with me, I think in a way he was glad to have someone to explain his ambitions to. 'Don't you see Billy, as I told you earlier, barristers can't go out and look for work, so if I want them to succeed I've got to do it for them, and that means that I've got to be seen around the courts, meet solicitors' clerks and try and get in amongst the good 'uns. Whenever one of our lot is in court I want to be there buzzing around him, making it look as if he's important. I want to try and find the young up-and-comings in case we've ever got any devilling for them, feed 'em with a bit of work, and then if they show promise and a vacancy occurs in these chambers, I've got them at least somewhere near the hook. It pays to be one or two jumps ahead in this business, Billy. Even in really good chambers, where you've got two prominent Silks and a couple of first rate barristers as juniors; where the cases are rolling in, and so is the money, suddenly your top two KCs can get preferments, be appointed as judges or the like, and you can find you're in trouble and way behind once again, unless you've safeguarded yourself by making sure you've got first class men to fill the vacancies all the way through. More than that, you've got to have made your own reputation as a first-rate clerk, one whose judgement is respected by solicitors, and who is known to do his best for everybody in his chambers and not one who just molly-coddles those at the top, and that kind of reputation is not gained by sitting on your arse in an office, which is why very soon I'm going to have to rely on you to look after things while I'm out.'

I was about to ask Packer for some further explanations when Mr Simmons and Mr Thin looked into the office, and told him they were leaving for lunch. They both deposited some for-midable-looking papers on his desk and asked him to see to them.

'Some work for you, me lad,' he said, as he glanced at them. I was apprehensive at this prospect, for although Packer had done a lot of talking he still hadn't got round to explaining my job. Again he seemed to read my thoughts, 'Don't worry, there's no urgency about these, they can wait until this afternoon, by which time I will have told you what you have to do with them. Now I too shall take my lunch and you can go for yours when I get back. While you're holding the fort you can make up the fires, and then think about what I've been telling you for if you've any questions now's the time to ask.'

His mentioning of the fires prompted me to ask about something that had been worrying me, in case it was a part of my duties. 'Who does the cleaning around here?' The discerning Packer chuckled, 'It's all right Billy, you don't, that's the job of the laundress.' 'I didn't mean who does the washing,' I replied, 'I meant the rooms.' At that he laughed even louder, 'You'll find out that here, Billy, words don't always mean what they should, even briefs can be long! Since the beginning of things in the Temple our cleaning women have been called laundresses. They are the only feminine society we have here, and you'll have to be up pretty early to meet them. They're part of a body of women that descend in hoards on the city and the West End from across the river every morning at about five. A lot of them don't look like women dressed in their caps, sack aprons and heavy boots, they seem like members of some strange race, but they're strong, Billy, you've got to be to carry buckets of coal up thirty steps every day, and they're not to be despised for if you ever do get up early enough to talk to them, they'll teach you a thing or two. Some families have been doing the same job for generations, they pass the jobs down from grandmother to mother, to daughter, and they know more about the history of the Temple than most of the lawyers. They can tell you all about the characters of the place and the changes that have taken place over the centuries. The only thing that hasn't changed it seems is their language, it's worse or better than Billingsgate, depending on your point of view.' With this he went off chuckling to his lunch. As he got to the door he took off his bowler and patted it. 'You won't forget this next time, will you Billy, eh?'

I don't think that before, or since, I ever felt so alone I dreaded a knock on the door, I wouldn't have known what to do or say to any caller. I thanked heaven that the telephone was seldom used, for I'd never spoken into one in my life. My brain too was reeling from the strain of trying to follow and understand even part of what Packer had said. I thought of what he'd told me about the duties and importance of a chief clerk, a position I supposed I would aspire to one day, though I couldn't for the life of me imagine myself in it. I still had to hear what my present job was to be and I could only trust that I would be able to do it. That reminded me that my immediate task was to make up the fires; at least it was something I knew how to do. I was now also able to take stock of the rooms; austere, august places, they all seemed alike, they had that same musty smell of learning that my headmaster's study had had, though the quantity and size of the books around the walls seemed to convey a wider and deeper knowledge. It seemed incredible that men could read so many books. I picked one from the shelves. As I blew the dust from it I thought 'this hasn't been opened for some time'. I looked inside and tried to read it, but quickly shut it and put it back on the shelf, my inability to understand it giving me an even greater feeling of inferiority. My attention was next drawn to a wig and gown hanging on a coat stand, the familiar marks of the barrister's profession. I'd seen them and sketched them from drawings in *Punch*, and I'd seen pictures of judges and barristers in the papers when some juicy murder or scandal case was being reported. I resisted the temptation to try the wig on, and since the fires were now burning brightly and I wasn't sure how long Packer would take over his lunch, I decided to return to his room.

I didn't have long to wait; he came back looking businesslike.

'No callers, eh? Good. Now you cut off and get your lunch, don't take too long about it and then we must put you to work.' I took him at his word and was back in minutes, having remembered to wear my bowler hat and to move at a seemly pace. 'Good lad,' he said approvingly, noticing my hat. Then he picked a bundle of papers off his desk. 'These,' he said, 'are Opinions,' and then he picked one off, 'that is Mr Simmons' statement on what he believes to be the fact, or the right course to be taken over a matter of law, which has been presented to him by a solicitor on behalf of a client. He may say "take no action-proceed, or settle out of court", and in each case give his reasons. Whichever it is this is what you have to copy out in your best handwriting on the inside of the back sheet. You will then return it to me and I shall take it to Mr Simmons for his signature. You will proceed in the same way with the rest of the bundle.' He then picked up another batch of papers. 'These', he said, 'are Pleadings, statements of cause; that is to say a matter about which a person goes to law, either in action, or defence, and they set out the way in which Mr Simmons will either prosecute or defend. Again all you have to do is to copy his instructions and return them to me. Have you got it?' I thought I had, so I nodded. It seemed simple enough, the sort of copybook stuff I had learned at school. Then I looked at the writing. Packer took my expression, 'Yes, that you will find is the hardest part of all, the deciphering. Many barristers believe that illegibility is the mark of their distinction. I believe doctors think the same way. In my opinion it's conceit, and a waste of your time and mine, and therefore a waste of their money, but in matters of this kind our opinion doesn't seem to concern them. It'll help you if I give you the translations done by your predecessor, but if you find you're in trouble, don't hesitate to ask me. Right, now sit down at that desk and get to work.'

'Have you got a pen for me?' I asked. 'Pen? Oh you mean a quill, you'll find one in the drawer of that desk.' I took one out and examined it gingerly. 'I've never used one of these before.' 'Oh you'll soon get used to them,' Packer replied, 'come over here and I'll show you how to cut one.' As he took out his penknife I realised for the first time how it had got its name. 'Now watch carefully, Billy, because this is another of your jobs. Every morning you will cut the quills for all the rooms.' I soon got the knack of it, and I found them easy enough to write with. I also got through my work satisfactorily if Packer's beaming expression as he examined it was anything to go by. His, 'Quite a good start, Billy,' when six o'clock came and he announced that I could go home, was also encouraging. As I was about to leave he called me back. 'There's one thing that I want to remind you of, and that is your promise to study shorthand and typing. Get yourself fixed up with evening classes as soon as possible, and work hard there. Despite what other people may say, it's going to be a necessary qualification before many years have passed, you mark my words.' He was right, as he was right about so many things. Packer was a go-getter, and although some of the other juniors that I later met told me I was unlucky to be in such a poor set of chambers, one thing was certain, I couldn't have had a better man to work under.

When I arrived back home that evening I was treated like the prodigal son and bombarded with questions; even my sister was interested to know how I had got on. It was hard to explain what I'd done, because though I'd copied quite a number of documents, I'd no idea what they meant. I'd just concentrated on getting the words down and spelt properly. I was able to describe the barristers, and to go into more detail about Mr Packer, though Mum had already told them how much she liked him.

So my days developed a routine. The hours of work were not hard, from 9.30 a.m. to 6 p.m., though occasionally it was necessary for me to stay later. On Saturdays, even though the Courts were closed, we worked until 2. On three evenings a week I attended night school, first at Sherbrook Road school, and later for more advanced classes at Childersley Street. My season ticket cost me 10 pence a week. I took a packed lunch of course. I gave Mum five shillings and had enough left for a whipped cream walnut every Saturday. If I wanted to go to the cinema or the halls Pop would take me, or give me the necessary money. I suppose my life could have become boring if it hadn't been for

Packer. He was determined to teach me everything he knew about the Law, and he seemed delighted at the progress I was making, particularly with my shorthand and typing. Whenever he could he'd dictate to me giving me the practice I needed, and it was a proud day for me when he announced in front of Mr Simmons that I was proficient enough for them to take advantage of my skill, and an even prouder one when he told me that it was his opinion that I was now more accomplished than he was. 'But you don't need to spread that around, Billy,' he warned me.

I learned to love the Temple, its buildings, lawns and gardens, that seemed to change with the light as well as with the seasons. When I later came to know the university towns of Oxford and Cambridge I found there the same atmosphere: the feeling of being in a place where the deep roots of wisdom and learning gave a dignity and permanence which would always survive the horrors, quarrels and pettinesses of the world outside. The Temple did change of course, slowly, almost unnoticeably between the wars. In chambers the soft light of the gas mantle gave way to the harsh electric bulb, though to this day the outside lighting is gas – the horse drawn cabriolet to the taxi. Later came the bombing of 1942, the post-war rebuilding, and finally the saturation of the cobbled squares by the automobile, which has given the Temple the garish appearance and the acrid smell of a car park. Even barristers now scurry to the law courts and if the sight of my mother pleased and excited Mr Simmons and Co., the wiggles of the mini-skirted typists would have driven them demented.

Again thanks to Packer, when things were slack I was allowed to attend the courts to see the end results of my work, and to listen to the forensic skills of the time. The law courts or Royal Courts of Justice were a minute or two's walk across Fleet Street from the Temple – 'Going over the way' we called it. They housed the High Court of Justice, which is divided into Chancery, where Equity cases are tried, that is cases which had no remedy in the old Common Law Courts; the King's Bench, which had replaced the old Common Law Courts, and where cases were tried by precedent, not by laws enacted by Parliament; and Probate, Divorce and Admiralty more easily described as 'Wills,

21

Wives and Wrecks'. These have recently been reorganized; Admiralty work now goes to the Queen's Bench Division, most Probate work to the Chancery Division, and the Divorce Division has been renamed the Family Division, though it still all adds up to the same thing. It wasn't until some time later that I visited the Old Bailey, the Central Criminal Court, and later still before I had the chance to see some of the Assize Courts, which are divided into seven circuits, the Northern, the North-Eastern, Midland, South-Eastern, the Oxford, the Western and Wales. These too have since changed their name, but not their job, and are now called Crown Courts. As Shakespeare might have said, 'What's in a name? the Villains still end up doing time.'

It was at the Royal Courts of Justice that I became familiar with many leading figures of the day, men like Marshall Hall, F. E. Smith, Patrick Hastings and Edward Carson. Marshall Hall's theatrical, almost melodramatic style was at that time beginning to lose its mesmeric grip on juries; and judges were also showing their impatience towards it, but it was still thrilling to me. I've already mentioned that F. E. Smith's chambers were above ours in Elm Court, though he was away in the services when I first joined, and it was not until later in 1915, when he was appointed Solicitor General in the Asquith government that he returned. I could always tell when he came into chambers, for he was an exception to Packer's rule, and ran in, bounding up the stairs two, sometimes three at a time. He shared chambers with his brother Harold, whom I found a charming man; whenever we met he greeted me with a smile and a good morning. F.E. was a different kettle of fish, he had no time for the likes of me. On some four or five occasions he ignored my 'Good morning, Sir' after which I gave up saying it, and never did he spare me a glance. This I found surprising since his own roots had been humble, and at one time he'd had a pronounced Lancashire accent. He got rid of it in six weeks when he was told that he couldn't expect any real advancement unless he learned to speak acceptable English. Whatever I may have thought of him at that time, there was no denying that he looked the part of a successful man. He was over

22

six feet tall, of handsome appearance and carried his clothes well, though some might have thought he was a bit dressy. He wore his hat on the back of his head, sported a buttonhole and he seemed always to have a long cigar in his mouth: if he didn't his lips drooped slightly open as though one should have been there. In court his forte was the cross-examination, though his arrogant and aggressive manner could put judge and jury against him; yet when later he addressed the jury, he soon put that to rights as his aggression turned to charm. It seemed he preferred the cut and thrust rather than the serious legal argument.

He was also one for the ladies, the drink and the high life. I became friendly with his junior clerk, and on terms with his chief, Mr Patel, so shared from time to time their gossip. They said he must have the stamina of an ox the way he combined work and play, without one interfering with the other. I had the opportunity of seeing the truth of this first hand, for one evening Mr Patel came into our office in a bit of a fluster. It was, he said, imperative that F.E. should receive certain papers that evening since they concerned a highly complicated 'Prize' case, in which he was appearing in the Admiralty Courts the following morning. I volunteered to take them. If the weight of the papers was anything to go by, the case had to be an intricate one. His butler opened the door, I explained my presence and handed him the papers. 'I will give them to him tomorrow morning,' the butler said. 'That will be too late,' I exclaimed, 'they're urgent, he has to appear in court at ten-thirty.' 'It's evident you don't know the way my master works. He has given me instructions that he is not to be disturbed this evening. At four o'clock tomorrow morning I shall wake him with a cup of black coffee. He will then study this case until eight, when he will take his breakfast, and I can promise you he will be in court fully informed, at the required time.' Somewhat relieved I bade him good evening, and made my way home.

Despite the butler's assurances I was anxious to hear how F.E. had got on, so the following evening I made my way upstairs and asked Mr Patel if everything had been satisfactorily concluded. 'Perfect, Billy, thank you, his arguments were quite brilliant.' I then told him what had happened and of my concern. He chuckled. 'Then you haven't heard the famous story about the Lever libel action of 1906. At that time F.E. was practising in Liverpool where he handled the legal business of Lever's the soap manufacturers. It was considered that the company had been libelled by the Northcliffe Press, and he received a telegram urgently requiring his presence in London. When he arrived at the Savoy Hotel that evening he was met by a solicitor, and immediately ushered to his room where there was a pile of books and papers about four foot high and he was told that an Opinion was required by the following morning. He ordered a bottle of champagne and two dozen oysters, and started to read. He worked throughout the night. At eight o'clock the following morning he wrote his Opinion. It was short and to the point. 'There is no answer to this action for libel, and the damages must be enormous – F.E. Smith.' His words were worth more than their weight in gold, for Northcliffe settled the case out of court for £50,000, the largest amount that had ever been paid in a libel action at that time.'

Another famous case that F.E. was concerned with was the Crippen Murder. He didn't appear in the doctor's trial, but later defended Ethel le Neve, Crippen's mistress, on a charge of being an accessory after the fact in the murder of his wife. It was an instance of the biter being bit, for he who could ignore so many people, was himself ignored. He was deeply wounded that she never gave or wrote a word of thanks for his successful defence.

Patel also showed me some of F.E.'s earlier Pleadings; unlike any of the barristers in our chambers he had excellent and clear handwriting. I remarked on this to Patel, who replied, 'I think it's because he treasures words, and is such a master in the use of them. You'll notice as you look through them, that you never have to read a sentence twice, its meaning is immediately clear.'

Perhaps F.E.'s most famous case came to trial while I was still at Elm Court. As Attorney General he prosecuted Roger Casement, the Irish patriot, for High Treason. It would have aroused intense public interest at that time anyway, but with the added ingredient of Casement's homosexual adventures as described in his diaries, it took over the headlines from all other incidents of the war. So much has been written and so much mud slung, some of which stuck to F.E., that it is unnecessary for me to enlarge on the case. I can only say that whoever had the task of prosecuting would almost certainly have come in for the same criticism, and I can report that the general opinion in the Temple at that time was that F.E. conducted his part in it courageously and fairly.

I've indicated that F.E. gave the impression that he breathed different air from other mortals, and that he was not as other men were. It came as a surprise and I think in a way as a delight to me to discover that he had feet of clay. One evening his junior clerk came down to our chambers sniggering. 'Come on upstairs,' he said, 'I've something to show you that I know you'll enjoy.' I followed him and he took me into F.E.'s office, and opening his desk took out an envelope which contained a number of saucy postcards. They weren't explicit by today's standards. My first reaction was that anyone who was so much in the company of that lovely actress Elsie Janis, shouldn't really need the stimulation of shadowy things, then I was rather pleased to think that this great man was really human, one of us, and I felt more warmly towards him. This was more than his clerk later felt. Unwisely he took the cards home with him that evening, and then to night school, where he showed them to his girlfriend. She snatched them from him, took them home and was discovered examining them by her mother. The cat was then really among the pigeons, and when she found where they had come from she could hardly be restrained from confronting F.E. Even now my mind boggles at the consequences of such an encounter.

Although I had left Elm Court when F.E. became Lord Chancellor, I was told of how he later rewarded Patel who had served him so well over the years. On his election to the Wool-sack he couldn't take his clerk with him. He must have known that Patel had hoped that eventually F.E. would be elected as a High Court Judge, and that, as was generally the case, he would go with him. F.E. bided his time, and when he broke with con-vention and appointed Edward Acton, then a County Court judge, to the High Court, he recommended Patel to join him as his clerk. It was an appointment that gave great satisfaction to both.

For me F.E. is an example of what can happen to a man who reaches the summit of success when comparatively young. He was forty-six when he took the Woolsack, and there is no doubt that he can be numbered among our great Lord Chancellors, but with a change of government, by the age of fifty he was as *The Times* said, 'Powerless, restless, almost alone.' He'd reached the end of the road. He was unable by law to return to the Bar and resume practice, even if he had wanted to. He took the appointment of Secretary of State for India in 1924, but was not satisfied by it. His extravagant private life now more and more filled the gap left by unfulfilled ambition, and he became a target for criticism from friends and enemies alike. There was a remarkable change in his appearance; his features quickly coarsened, and the dress of a man who was once such a dandy now became casual, almost sloppy. This indifference was also noticeable in his personal financial dealings. When he left politics in 1928 for the City, he had six cars, a yacht, three chauffeurs, eight horses and three grooms, a town and a country house, and a huge overdraft, yet if he was reprimanded for his extravagance he was likely to respond by buying yet another car, or something equally expensive. He died in 1930, at the age of fifty-nine, a time when many men begin to come to power and high position. I wondered then and I do now, whether, if his success had been slower, less mercurial, he wouldn't have made a finer and greater contribution to public and political life, and have lived a deal longer.

Because of my visits to the Courts I got to know the attendants there, indeed I went out of my way to develop their acquaintance, for as Packer told me, they could help to oil the wheels when we were appearing there. A Mr Pearce was the head at that time; a great character who made his own rules and changed them when it suited him. He told me that in his opinion one of his ushers should have appeared in the Courts himself for fraud, for whenever this man escorted visitors around he would pause by a certain table, which he had previously decorated with quill pens, probably purchased the same day from Partridge and Cooper on the corner of

Chancery Lane. 'These, ladies and gentlemen, are some of our most famous pens,' he would say. 'It was this one that signed the death warrant of Doctor Crippen', and if there was an American present, 'This one our Ambassador to your country Lord Reading used. You'd like to see it, Sir?' Then a whispered conversation would take place about how as a special favour he might take it as a memento of his visit. 'Perhaps you'll wait behind afterwards, Sir, I'm sure it can be arranged.' And arranged it was, money was passed and another pen put in its place awaiting the next party of visitors. Come to think of it, anyone who wanted that kind of souvenir deserved everything he got.

It is strange now, how little impression the war made on me at that time. I suppose it was partly because none of my near relations were at the front, and that my contemporaries in the Temple were too young to think about life in the services. Although we were aware that things were not going all our way, somehow we never contemplated defeat, and indeed thought that victory, like love, was just around the corner. An occasional reminder of the savagery of the fighting came if ever I had to walk to Trafalgar Square. A glance down Villiers Street would show a line of ambulances waiting to collect the wounded from Charing Cross station. The war had affected Packer who had tried to enlist but who had failed to pass the medical because of the stomach complaint he had described in such detail to my mother at our first meeting. He had been given the white feather once or twice, and had been jeered at by returning troops at Waterloo station. As he'd told Mum, he was a keen cricketer; he played for Honor Oak, and many Saturdays he would bring his bag to the Temple, so that he could get to his game after work. If ever his journey meant that he had to catch a train from a main line station, he would ask me to carry his bag for him since, as he said, he couldn't put up with the barrage of abuse that he met at Waterloo from soldiers and their relatives. 'If you're fit enough to play bloody cricket, you're fit enough to be in the trenches.'

It was cricket that got Packer into the kind of trouble that clerks' nightmares are made of. He had persuaded Mr Simmons to allow him to play on a weekday. It was a match that had something to do with lawyers because Cheeseman, then clerk to Lord Jowett, and Mark Ostrer, a managing clerk to B. A. Wolfe & Co., a firm of solicitors, were also playing and travelling with him. Apparently the game went well, but in the excitement Packer had forgotten to study the lists – that is the diary of cases coming to court, and one of ours was missed and in the absence of any lawyers was struck out. All hell was let loose. Packer had to sign an affidavit to the effect that it was entirely his fault, but that wasn't enough for the judge. He had him in court, gave him a thorough dressing down and ended by saying that all the costs of the postponement would have to be paid by us as clients. Packer didn't try and make excuses either to the judge, to Mr Simmons or to the solicitors. In those days excuses were not acceptable, and indeed would have only made matters worse. As it was there were dark clouds round our office for days, and cricket was not a word to mention.

Mark Ostrer, one of Packer's team mates on that day, was a man who later became a leader of the British film industry, and with his brother Isadore helped to found the Gaumont British Picture Corporation. Isadore was the financier with a brilliant mind and the ability to negotiate; Mark was the front man, a man of charm, who could socialize and drink champagne with the greatest of them. At that time, as a managing clerk, he was responsible for arranging his solicitors' court work, and was probably earning no more than thirty shillings a week. When Mark gave up the law Packer saw no more of him for a few years, then one day he turned up at Elm Court with a strange request; he had been summoned for jury service, and wanted Packer's advice as to how he could best get out of it. The advice was given, it worked and didn't cost Mark a penny. As a reward Packer received a special pass which allowed him a free seat in any Gaumont British cinema, at any time.

Apart from this one serious lapse, Packer, in my experience, never put a foot wrong. Within a year of my joining him he had in large part succeeded in doing what he had outlined to me on my first day. Work did come flowing, so much so that he was able to push a lot of it in the direction of Colin Duncan, as well as providing devilling work for young up-and-comings. Duncan was the odd man out in an otherwise Jewish chambers. There was at that time in the Temple, and indeed in some chambers there still is, a kind of Masonry. There were Catholic, Jewish, Irish and English Protestant chambers and most of the work came from solicitors of a similar persuasion. This did not of course apply to the more brilliant barristers whose Opinions and Pleadings were sought when it was considered necessary, and if the clients could afford them. There were also those chambers where it was possible for the chief clerk to pick and choose, taking in only those barristers whom he considered were likely quickly to succeed, and whom he thought would eventually rise to the top of their profession. Packer was one of these, he didn't particularly like having a predominantly Jewish chambers, he wanted men on their merits and this was why he fostered Duncan who was well on the way to the top, when, tragically, he died of cancer.

Other successes that Packer had later were Gilbert Paul, who became a fine judge, R. F. Levy, one-time Chairman of the Monopolies Commission, and Mr Justice Marshall, the judge in the notorious Stephen Ward case, who indirectly was responsible for Ward's death. Stephen Ward it was who introduced Mr Profumo, the then Minister of Defence, to Christine Keeler, the prostitute who was to bring about Profumo's ultimate disgrace and resignation. Ward was charged with a variety of offences, such as conspiring to procure abortions, and living off the earnings of prostitutes. Justice Marshall's summing up was obviously a direction for the jury to find Ward guilty, and, as it was concluded at the end of the day, the jury had no time to retire or to give their verdict. Yet Ward was allowed to return home with the know-ledge that he was bound to be convicted, so rather than face the consequences he poisoned himself. In circumstances of that kind it is the duty of the judge to see that the accused is kept in custody overnight. Judge Marshall failed in that duty. His career, however, should not be assessed on that case alone, for if judges didn't make mistakes there would be no need for the Court of Appeal. It was one, though that had a particularly wretched ending, and there were many who thought that Stephen Ward's conviction

29

might well have been quashed on appeal.

It was inevitable that Packer's enthusiasm and drive influenced my attitude towards work; and the way in which he was able to get fun and enjoyment out of practically any situation almost certainly had an effect on my approach to the Law, and indeed on my whole philosophy of life. He was a person I found it easy to identify with, his ways became my ways. I owe him a lot.

Although he didn't know it, he was responsible for me leaving Elm Court. When I realised I was more than proficient at short-hand and typing I put in for a rise in salary. I didn't overdo it, I felt I now deserved ten shillings a week. Packer agreed, and put it to Simmons. It was refused. I was disappointed but not downcast. I checked around the Temple and found that the going rate for boys with my qualifications was even higher than my own estimate of myself. I also knew that with more young men being drawn into the war, there was a shortage of junior clerks of some experience. I put it around amongst my fellows that I might be interested in a change, but was careful to see that it didn't get to Packer's ears. Someone suggested to me that I saw 'Old Worthy', who was clerk to the Bar Council, and who kept a register of those barristers who were looking for clerks. 'What old worthy,' I asked. 'That's his name, Worthy – Mr Worthy.' When I met him he looked his name, a venerable old man, sitting on a high stool and smoking a hooked pipe, for all the world like the caterpillar in *Alice in Wonderland*. I told him what I was there for and gave him an account of my experience. Taking his pipe from his lips, and wiping his mouth with handkerchief, he said, 'Why look further, I want a clerk here.' I stammered out a trifle too quickly that I wanted to be a barrister's clerk. 'All right, all right,' he said, edgily, 'I just thought you might be interested.' He then asked me how much money I expected. I said I thought a pound. He repeated my words as he wrote in his register, 'Sydney Aylett, he thinks a pound.' 'Right,' he said, 'that will be all. If I hear of anything I will send someone round to see you.' I left him feeling discouraged; nothing, I said to myself, is likely to come from that quarter.

I was wrong. About a couple of weeks later I received a note from a Mr Dobson, asking if I would call on him at Number 4 Paper Buildings, Lord Robert Cecil's chambers, during my lunch break that day. When I arrived there there was a man standing outside who stopped me as I was about to go in. 'Mr Aylett?' 'Yes.' 'I'm Dobson, perhaps we could have a little chat. We'll sit on that bench over there, if you don't mind.' The situation had begun to take on an air of a spy thriller. 'I understand from Mr Worthy that you wish to better your position,' he began. 'What are your qualifications?' And so the rigmarole started again. When I got to my proficiency in shorthand and typing he grunted. 'You'll need the shorthand, but they'll never allow a typing machine in these chambers.' Eventually he rose to his feet, 'Well,' he said, 'I think you'll do.' It struck me as a very strange and abrupt way to conduct business. 'What about money?' I asked. 'Oh you'll have to ask Wootton about that,' he replied. 'Who is he?' 'Why the chief clerk of course.' 'Then who are you?' 'Oh, I am only the departing junior, but Wootton asked me to find someone I could recommend to take my place, and now I've found you. Why, who did you think I was?' When I told him I'd taken him for the chief clerk, he laughed. 'Well I suppose I very nearly am one,' he said. 'I'm joining Sir Henry Fielding Dickens' chambers as chief in a fortnight's time. His clerk has gone into the army. Dickens' chambers are also in Paper Buildings, so I shan't be far away if ever you need any help. You'll find Wootton spends quite a bit of his time out of chambers, not looking for work I hasten to add, that's not necessary, it comes rolling in. You may have a bit of trouble with some of the writing, Macnaghten's isn't too bad, but Mathew's is like a spider.'

There was one other thing that interested me. 'Is Sir Henry any relation to Charles Dickens, the writer?' 'Yes, he's the second son. It's a bit odd really when you consider some of the nasty things his father wrote about lawyers.' 'When shall I come to see Mr Wootton?' I asked. 'I should come round about six this evening, he should be in then. If it's not convenient, I'll drop a note round to you.'

Apparently it was convenient, so I made my way to Number 4

Paper Buildings at the appointed time. The chambers were one of a pair on the ground floor. I knocked on the door, which immediately swung open, though to my surprise there was no one on the other side. As I went in there was a voice from the end of the passage which called, 'Come along down here.' I followed it into a small room, where a short, plump Dickensian figure, aged around forty-five, greeted me from behind a desk. 'You'll be Aylett. Hm, you look a bit worried, boy.' 'I was wondering how that door managed to open.' 'Ah, I see you've an enquiring mind. Well since we don't like wasting time or energy here, we rigged up this device,' and he pointed to two cords hanging near his desk. 'With a few pulleys and a deal of ingenuity, we've arranged it that one lifts the latch, and the other pulls the door open. Well now lad, let's get down to business. What's your Christian name?' I told him, and launched yet once again into my *curriculum vitae*. My typewriting skill came in for the same comment, 'You'll never use it in these chambers while Mr Mathew is here. He hates machines. If he had his way there'd be no telephone.'

Eventually he asked me for a sample of my handwriting, and I copied from a Pleading he gave me. He seemed satisfied. 'Now what about money?'

'I want a pound a week,' I said, firmly. I didn't say, 'I was thinking about a pound' this time. He seemed a bit shaken. 'Hm, let's say eighteen shillings, shall we, it isn't a lot less but it sounds better, or it will do to them in there,' he said, gesturing down the corridor. I agreed. He then left me, taking with him the specimen of my handwriting. I heard him enter and leave two of the rooms before he returned. 'It all seems quite satisfactory. I'll now take you in to meet them.' I went first to meet Mr Malcolm Macnaghten, who rose, shook my hand and wished me well. Then to Theobald Mathew, who gazed at me from under his pince-nez spectacles and made polite noises at me. I couldn't have been in either room for more than thirty seconds. 'Well, my lad, that's that then, it seems you suit. Now when will you be able to join us?' asked Wootton. I explained that I had to give a fortnight's notice, and it was agreed that I should start immediately I had seen my time out. When I informed Packer of my impending departure he was not at all pleased. It was not that he disapproved of my motive, 'I can understand you wanting to get more money, Billy, and I know they turned you down on that score here, but you should have asked for my advice and help. You might have done better if you had.' Still when the time came for me to go he shook me by the hand and told me I'd always be a welcome visitor. So I left Simmons' chambers with mixed feelings. I was pleased to be getting so much more money, but I wasn't sure about Wootton, it seemed to me he didn't compare with Packer, and I hadn't really been impressed with the two barristers I'd met. 'Oh well,' I thought, 'I can but give it a try.' I tried it for fifty-seven years, and enjoyed every one of them.

Chapter Three

Since I was to spend over half a century at Number 4, I will describe Paper Buildings. It was, and still is, a set of chambers in an oblong block, north-east of the Inner Temple Gardens, whose lawns lead down from Crown Office Row to the Embankment. It was built in 1610 and was officially called Heywards Building, but because it was constructed of timber, lath and plaster, known in the trade as 'paper work', the block was dubbed with its name, and it stuck.

Numbers 1 to 4 were burned down in 1838, and were rebuilt by a Mr Smirke, and Number 5 was added ten years later. There is an inscription on one of the walls, and I was told that, during the re-building, one of the masons had asked the Treasurer of the Temple if he wanted anything inscribed on the wall. The treasurer at the time was engrossed in other important matters, and replied sharply, 'Be gone about your business'. The mason took him at his words. There was an occasion when the name of the building took on another significance. I remember an angry and dissatisfied client emerging from one of the offices saying, 'I now understand why you live at this address, you're all paper and no action.' I hasten to add that dissatisfied clients were rare at Number 4.

There are two examples in the Inner Temple Gardens of lawyers' ability to laugh at themselves. Near the southern end of Paper Buildings is a sundial which was presented originally to Clement's Inn by Lord Clare. It is in the form of a kneeling black boy, holding a platter with an inscription that reads:

In vain, poor sable son of woe,
Thou see'st the tender tear;
From cannibals thou fled'st in vain,
Lawyers less quarter give;
The first won't eat you till you're slain.
The last will do it alive.

At a nearby pond is another statue of a boy, which bears the words: 'Lawyers were children once.'

To describe the inside of our chambers at Number 4 is both simple and difficult. It is simple to say that there were four rooms of decreasing size, of which Wootton and I shared the smallest; but it is difficult to say anything interesting about their furnishings, or contents. A barrister's room is after all an office, and though I'm told today that some chief executives furnish theirs lavishly and expensively, in those days, and indeed in all my time at the Temple, there was the feeling that it was unwise to give any indication of wealth, otherwise clients might feel that they were being fleeced; as it was they complained loud enough.

I knew that my first job was to get to know, and be on terms with, Mr Wootton. It was on him that my destiny depended. It wasn't difficult. He was a nice enough codger, though very different from Packer. It was as though security had made him complacent, almost lazy. He was in charge of a set of chambers where all the members were busy and successful; he felt he didn't have to go out and look for work. In a way he was right, but as Packer had said, and I was to find out later for myself, no matter how busy you are in chambers, it pays always to be in the front line, find out who the up-and-comings are among both barristers and solicitors. You should know who specializes in what kind of cases, so that when asked by a solicitor or his clerk whom you can recommend, you can nominate the right man even if he's not in your chambers; though if he's not you make sure that he hears of your recommendation. You have to know whom to go to for your devilling. You must be able to recognize the idiosyncracies and peculiarities of judges, and the strengths and weaknesses of opposing counsel, so that you can pass your knowledge on to young barristers.

When I told Packer of my first impression of Wootton, he rubbed his hands with glee. 'Splendid, Sydney,' (he paid me the compliment of calling me by my proper name for the first time), 'now if you take my tip you'll turn his weaknesses to your advantage. Do all the things he doesn't do, work hard, and seize every occasion you can to get around outside. Make yourself as indispensable as possible; the more you do the more Wootton will push on to you, and it won't go unnoticed in chambers or elsewhere, so that eventually you'll be wearing his shoes without him knowing it, and when the time comes for him to go you will automatically take his place.'

George Wootton, or as he constantly and irritatingly referred to himself, 'George Washington, never tell a lie, Wootton,' was a man of habit. He would arrive at the office at precisely 9.45 each morning, take off his coat or mackintosh, and in winter his galoshes, put his coat on a hanger, then he would remove his hat, revolve it in his hands, and if he thought it necessary, would expel either rain or dust with the clothes brush which hung on a hook nearby; finally, having adjusted his tie, he would raise himself onto his chair and with a sigh pick up the day's mail and say piously, 'Father forgive them, for they know not what they do.' As he read the mail he would emit the occasional chuckle, 'That should be a nice one,' and would put it on one side so that he could comment on it when he later took them into the rooms. After the post had been cleared and distributed he would make sure that I had plenty to occupy my time, before he began scratching around the place like an old hen. At five to eleven precisely, he would pick up an envelope and with a, 'Must make sure this letter gets delivered,' he would put on his coat and hat and make his way to a pub in Tudor Street.

I only knew this, of course, by hearsay, he never asked me to join him. After he'd had his drink he would then take a walk round all the pubs and eating houses, to study their menus for the day. When he'd made his selection he would return – it would then be about midday – and inform me that I could go for my lunch; with my increase in salary I could now afford a hot midday meal. I was expected to return within half an hour, which gave him two hours for his own lunch. I think he knew that his long absence would not be noticed, since counsel would be taking theirs at the same time. He came back at about half-past two looking rubicund and jolly, but by now he'd got a real taste for the drink, so at five to three he'd slip out for another, without worrying about giving an excuse. At a quarter past three he would return and resign himself to doing a bit more work. Then at ten to five he 'stepped over the way', meaning the Royal Courts of Justice, which meant another session at the pub, until half past six, by which tine the barristers started to leave for home. Theo Mathew was always the last. It was a quarter past seven before he opened his room and bade us goodnight. His timekeeping at times infuriated Wootton, who would pace up and down the corridor hoping to attract attention to the lateness of the hour. It was wasted effort, Theo Mathew was a law unto himself. It was also a law that we could not leave until the barristers had.

Although the picture I've drawn of George makes him out to be a near alcoholic, I was quite fond of him. He could be highly astute at times, particularly when pricing a brief, and could screw money out of the stoniest of solicitors. I think his home life was a bit severe and that he had one of those wives who made him seek his pleasures during working hours. He occasionally dropped remarks about the hardness of women, and the dangers of matrimony. I remember one day he came back to the office in the afternoon with a suit that he had had made for him. He was very proud of it, he changed into it in the office and strutted up and down in front of me asking my opinion. It was a black and white small check; although I thought it was going it a bit, he cut quite a dash in it and I told him so – pleased as Punch he was. The next morning he came to the office with the suit in a parcel. He saw me raising my eyebrows. 'I'm not having it. Sydney, it's no good, no good at all, makes me look like Harry Champion, or some sort of bookie. It won't do, it's going back.' It was as if he was repeating what someone else had told him, and it made me feel sad. I knew he would have loved to have kept it.

I had cause to be less than friendlily disposed towards Mrs Wootton. There was a butcher's, Spears and Pond, near the Temple, and one day old George, whose mind was never far away from his stomach, saw that they were selling ox tails, which were 'off the ration'; food rationing was in force by then, so he bought one and took it home in great glee to his wife. He found he'd started something; from then on she expected him to make a similar contribution to the table each week. He soon got tired of what were often fruitless calls at the butcher's, so the job was passed on to me. 'While you're out, Sydney, go round to Spears and Pond, and see if they've got anything today,' he'd say as I left for lunch. The assistant there took it out on me, 'Here comes Oliver bloody Twist, nothing more for you today, son,' he'd jeer. One day he offered me a hare. This was a great prize. He handed it to me by the legs. 'Aren't you going to wrap it up?' I asked. 'Not likely, lad, can't spare the paper.' I felt a proper narner, all five foot five of me, carrying that hare along Fleet Street and into the Temple, with its nose just an inch off the ground. I heard one wag of a barrister as he passed, saying to his companion, 'The Lincoln's Inn poacher, I presume.'

A couple of months later George was to have an experience that outdid my hare episode. Lord Robert Cecil had lodged a bid at Stevens, the autioneers in Covent Garden, for a human skeleton. He wanted it for a young friend or relation who was studying medicine. His bid was successful, and he asked George to collect the 'remains'. They were packed, it seemed, quite well, in a wooden box, some two feet long. Since it provided him with an excuse to be away from the office, George was only too pleased to accept. Whether he'd had a drink or two on the way and so handled the box carelessly, or whether, as he said, the lock gave way, we shall never know, but as he was about to cross the Strand the lid came open, and the 'remains' scattered across the road. Women screamed, horses reared, and George was manhandled until a policeman arrived on the scene and he was able to tell his story. By then a considerable crowd had collected, and when at last he had cleared himself in the eyes of the law, they helped him to gather the bones and to sling them back into the box; though not without many coarse comments. Then when he set off again, one or two of the jokers, with nothing better to do, followed him, shouting, 'Make way for Doctor Crippen.' By the time he returned to chambers George was in a very nasty state. He dumped the box in our office, and announced briefly, 'I'm off home, if his lordship puts in an appearance, tell him his bones are there.' Lord Robert didn't come in, so the following morning George and I went through the box, did some minor repair work and made the skeleton more presentable, while he related his story to me. He could now see the funny side of it. So could Theo Mathew, who when he saw what we were doing, remarked wryly, 'The lawyers pick the flesh, but leave the bones for their clerks.'

There was another time when Lord Robert was to cause further embarrassment to his chief clerk. It was his lordship's habit to travel from chambers to Parliament on a tricycle. One day he summoned George to the House of Lords, and, as it was an important occasion, he wore his frock coat and silk top hat. When their business was concluded, Lord Robert asked George if he would return the tricycle to chambers as he was travelling home direct from the House, but would need his machine at the Temple the following morning. At first George tried pushing the thing, but his top hat kept falling over his eyes, so he mounted it. It wasn't as easy to ride as it looked, and as he was wobbling along the front wheel hit some horse manure, the bike skidded, overturned and George bit not just the dust, but the horse manure. Fortunately only his dignity and his frock coat were hurt, but his appearance and aroma attracted the attention of passers-by, and once again he was chi-iked all the way back to the Temple. George took against that tricycle from then on, and I noticed that if he saw it standing outside Paper Buildings, he would give it a surreptitious little kick as he passed.

George seemed to attract discomfort as jam attracts wasps. One day, around lunch time, I'd been sent to get a cab for one of our clients. Every one I hailed was occupied, and it was some twenty minutes before I was able to return to chambers. My patience and resolution went unrewarded, except with grumbles and grunts about the time I'd taken. I remarked on this to Wootton. 'You were lucky', he responded, 'I remember when I was with Lord Russell in the chambers he'd taken in New Court, Carey Street. He demanded that I get him a hansom cab to take him to Kensington, "Get me one with a strong, high stepping horse, I've some heavy books to take with me," he added, as I left. Now I knew that on that particular day cabbies were striking for better pay, and were refusing to accept any long trips. I also knew that it was no good telling Lord Russell that; he would still have told me to go and get one. I did succeed in stopping a couple, but when I told them where they'd got to go, they quickly made off, so I changed my tactics and pretended that the destination was Charing Cross Station. The cabbie was a sullen-looking brute, but eventually he agreed to accept the fare; then I saw his horse, a half-starved, mangy flea-bitten nag, that didn't look as though it would get as far as Charing Cross, let alone Kensington, which was, I hoped, to be its eventual destination. When we reached New Court I hopped out and was irritably greeted by his lordship, who hadn't enjoyed being kept waiting. Then he saw the horse, "What the devil do you call this, George?" he cried, "I asked for a high stepper, not a candidate for the knacker's yard." I wasn't called upon to reply to that, the cabbie took over. It was in the "Don't you talk to me like that, my man, or I'll call the police and put you in charge for insultin' language and behaviour," days, so eventually, knowing what was good for him, the cabbie quietened down. Lord Russell then signalled me to put the pile of books into the cab. As I did this I saw the horse being lifted out of its harness, and when his lordship got inside it seemed as though the wretched animal was propelled into the air. At last they set off, I heaved a sigh of relief, and went back into chambers. It wasn't the end of the tale. The next morning I was summoned into his lordship's room, "You owe me a sovereign, George," he said. "You told that cabbie to drive to Charing Cross, when I wanted him to go to Kensington." I tried to explain. "No excuses, George, that frightful fellah took me to the station, and refused to budge until I coughed up. Now you can do the same." When finally I was allowed to explain what

I had done – and why – his lordship took it in better part, but ever after that I looked at the horse first before hailing a cab for him, to make sure that I got a high stepper.'

Dear old George, though I was never on the same terms with him as I had been with Packer he was good company, despite the fact that I had to do most of his work for him. As for his habit of always trying to go one better, I got a deal of amusement out of it and found myself inventing imaginary situations, which I would recount as personal experiences just to test and enjoy his creative powers. One I didn't have to invent concerned my prowess at dancing, which for a time became my main diversion; it also provided a means to an end – meeting young ladies. I was telling him how I'd learned some particular step, but didn't get very far, 'Ah, dancing, yes, it was something I excelled at when I was your age. My wife and I were great exponents of the waltz – it was considered quite daring in my young day. Very proficient we became, won many prizes, you know.' I must say that as I looked at that plump little figure, I found it hard to believe, and even more difficult when that same afternoon I met Mrs Wootton for the first, and only, time. She was even fatter than her husband, though she was contained in corsets. The idea of them floating round the ballroom to the strains of the Blue Danube made my imagination boggle.

Although Lord Robert Cecil was the head of chambers at Number 4, it was not to be my good fortune to see much of him, nor to work for him because his parliamentary duties meant that he was rarely with us. What little I did see I liked. He was a man in his early fifties, a tall impressive figure, gaunt with a beak-like Cecil nose and long upper lip. He spoke beautifully; hearing him gave me as much pleasure as listening to a concert singer. Just before I joined he had been appointed as Minister of Blockade, a position which he held until the end of the war. After the Armistice we all hoped he would return to chambers, none more than Wootton, for Coward, Chance & Co., an important firm of solicitors, called on him to see if he would take a brief for the Rajahs, during the settlement of the Indian Boundaries, and offered a vast fee. Lord Robert turned it down because of his

41

government work, and eventually became President of the League of Nations Union, Lord Privy Seal and Chancellor of the Duchy of Lancaster.

I once met another member of the Cecil family. I was alone in chambers one afternoon, when an elderly gentleman, sporting a white moustache, came in and asked for Lord Robert. I told him that I thought he was at the House, but he replied that he understood that he would be calling in shortly, and did I mind if he waited. He stood there chatting to me for the best part of half an hour, showing a knowledge of, and a great interest in, the Law, and in particular in the part I played. Finally, he said that as it didn't look as if his lordship had been able to keep the appointment, he would be on his way. 'Who shall I say called?' 'Oh tell him it was his brother – Salisbury.' I was bowled over, my eyes went straight to his nose, there it was, the beak that I should have recognised. 'Very well, my Lord,' I murmured, and he bade me a good-afternoon. For me it had been a good one, for I'd spent half an hour chatting with the Marquis of Salisbury – the King Maker.

When eventually Lord Robert decided to vacate his room, he left behind two things that I was able to keep, his clothes brush and his black felt hat. I'm afraid I didn't give the hat the respect it deserved for by now, like my father, I was engaging in theatricals, and I used it as a prop in a knock-about sketch I occasionally performed.

In writing about Lord Robert I may have given the idea that my opinion of him was swayed by what he was, an aristocrat and a great public figure. This was not wholly the case; of course as a teenager I was impressed to meet, what at any rate to me, were the great people in the land, but what particularly astonished me was that the higher they were in birth or position, the more ordinary and approachable they were as people; tolerant and kind, with time to spare; never distant, class-conscious or superior. People may jeer at the jingoism of Kipling's poem, 'If', but I saw the qualities he wrote of in the characters of men, particularly when I was young. I think they have been eroded as I have grown older, though two of my latter-day heroes, Kenneth Diplock and

Quintin Hogg, were notable exceptions. At the risk of giving offence I find it hard to see the logic of demanding the highest breeding in horses and other animals, yet dismissing such a practice when applying it to men and women.

Malcolm Macnaghten was the man I was to work closest with during my first few years in the new chambers. He was forty-seven when I joined, and my first impression of him, as more a bishop than a lawyer, never changed. He was quiet, charming and unassuming. He was an Ulster Unionist Member of Parliament from 1922–8. His speech was musical and persuasive although he was inclined to stammer a little. It wasn't the mannerism that I have learned to associate with Etonians and guards officers, who I believe adopt it because it gives them an extra second or two to think before replying, neither was it an indication of nervousness, nor did it affect his advocacy or irritate judges, for he was a great favourite with the judiciary.

What I wrote earlier, that barristers often had to wait up to five years for their first brief, did not apply to the sons of judges. They had a much easier time of it. To begin with their fathers could afford to give them a reasonable allowance, and gave it without question, since they knew from experience how necessary it was. Solicitors and barristers were also quick to know which judge was friendly with whom, so that if they introduced a son as a junior, in certain circumstances it might give their case an easier ride. But if the boy doesn't succeed, or isn't ready, then he's back to square one. It can, however, be of great help in giving youth the start and confidence it needs; for in many cases the man in the dock is not the only one who is shivering with fear. Opposing counsel have also been known to go carefully with judges' sons.

But having said this, and following it with the fact that Macnaghten was the fourth son of Lord Macnaghten, one of the greatest legal brains of all time, I do not mean that he owed his success to any kind of nepotism. Although he was nicknamed 'Muggins' at Eton, he was far from being one. He won a major scholarship to Trinity College, Cambridge, was President of the Union, and gained a first class honours degree in history. His main work, when I joined, was with Privy Council cases. He'd been lucky as a result of the war, for he took over Geoffrey Lawrence's, later Lord Lawrence, practice, much of which was Privy Council work. He handed it back after the war of course, but some of it stuck.

In court his quiet manner persisted, he was charming to judges and witnesses alike. He never hectored or bullied, yet nevertheless succeeded in getting at the truth, and he was able to expound his arguments to juries, simply and directly. It was the popular style, the swing of the pendulum from Marshall Hall and his like. It was my opinion that he got away with a great deal through his gentlemanly conduct. He took Silk in 1919. F.E. Smith was the Lord Chancellor who presented him and when he came to Macnaghten he said, 'Malcolm Macnaghten, it is with great pleasure that I give to you, the son of a great father, a King's Councillor's gown.' Like so many barristers before and since, Macnaghten's work dropped sharply when he became a leader; John Simon, later Chancellor of the Exchequer and Lord Chancellor, was the man whose services were then in demand in Privy Council cases. Still it was a necessary step towards the High Court judgeship, which was Macnaghten's goal.

It was after the war that I achieved a great breakthrough, by finally persuading Macnaghten and Theo Mathew to buy a typewriter for the chambers. It was to make work faster and easier for me, though early on I had my doubts when Macnaghten kept dictating letters to clients, 'Now we have a typewriter in chambers I find I can allow myself to become more loquacious.' And he did! Another great day in all our lives at Paper Buildings was when electric lighting was installed there. Mathew found the installation interrupted his work, and spoke about it as an unnecessary evil. But when everything was completed and the electrician was ready to switch the power on, an excited little group had gathered for the occasion. As the lights went on there was a gasp, and the electrician cried above it, 'Thank God! It works.'

It was early in the 1920s that I helped Macnaghten, who had been knighted for political and public services, draw up the present boundaries between Northern and Southern Ireland. I suppose

44

today, anyone employed on or near such work would have to sign the Official Secrets Act, and the papers would have to be guarded day and night. As it was, all Sir Malcolm said was, 'You'll have to keep mum over this, Sydney, not a word to a soul.' In a way it was quite an unnecessary order, for I couldn't make head nor tail of it. I just wrote down what I was told, and bought a book about Ireland so that I could make sure of spelling the names of the places correctly. In 1924 Sir Malcolm was appointed as Recorder to Colchester. A recorder is a paid judicial position, a cross between a magistrate and high court judge. He held both criminal and civil juridiction over courts and quarter sessions. It wasn't until another four years had passed that Sir Malcolm was eventually elected as a High Court Judge. There were fewer such appointments made in those days, indeed, I believe I am right in saying that no other judge had been created during those four years. It was to be a red letter day in my life when he accepted the preferment, because at that time it was the custom that when the head of chambers was elected to the judiciary he took with him his chief clerk as judge's clerk, and this meant that Wootton would be leaving our chambers. The question now was whether I would be chosen to succeed him, or would I, at the age of twenty-eight, be considered too young and inexperienced, and someone else be elected from another chambers? I won the day; but this takes me ahead of my story.

Sir Malcolm took his election with humility and some trepidation. One morning, shortly after he had received the news, I found him in his room holding his pocket watch in front of him. 'Come over here, Sydney, and draw up a chair.' He moved the watch between the two of us. 'Can you hear it ticking?' he asked. I told him I could. 'Well I can't.' Then he held it closer to himself, 'Can you hear it now?' Again my answer was yes. He put the watch back in his pocket. 'I'm worried, my boy, about my hearing, I've been to my doctor, who tells me it's just *anno domini*, but I don't want to be one of those judges who get branded as deaf old buffers. Are there any ideas you have that I can use to avoid it.' As it happened I had one or two, 'Whatever you do, Sir, don't start putting your hand to your ear, or that will

45

give the game away. Make an arrangement with your associate (that is the person who does the swearing in of the witnesses and sits beneath the judge) so that whenever you're unsure of what has been said from the box, you can consult him, without having to ask what was said. He will then tell you. It was a dodge Justice Horridge used to employ, and it seemed to work very well. After that you can just turn back to the box and instruct the witness to carry on. You'll also find, Sir, that it will become second nature to you to know whether a witness has said anything of importance, or not.' Sir Malcolm was grateful and told me he would try and follow my advice. I don't know whether he did, but I do know that I never heard anyone criticising him for his deafness. If it had happened it would soon have become common knowledge in the Temple.

Perhaps encouraged by my answer, he then asked me if I had any other advice to offer him. 'Speak out, Sydney,' he said, as I hesitated, 'I don't mind what you say about me.'

'Well Sir, it's those high collars you wear, they are old fashioned, and if you'll pardon me for saying so, they don't become you.' I was referring to the starched two-and-a-half-inch-wide collars that went right round the neck, rather like a parson's collar only more so. He seemed a bit put out by my remark. 'I'll think about it, Sydney,' he replied. A couple of days later he called me into his room. He was wearing a winged court collar. 'Is this more to your liking, Sydney?' he asked with a smile. 'Well I must say I think it suits you better, Sir, and you look years younger,' I replied. 'Those were my wife's words, my boy, so it seems you were right after all,' he commented.

It was when we came to say goodbye that it was Sir Malcolm's turn to give me counsel. Having thanked me, and congratulated me on my appointment as Chief Clerk, he paused for a moment, and then said, 'There's one piece of advice that I would like to give you in your new capacity. Don't ask for too high fees. I think you will find shortly that the economy won't stand them, and I believe it will be everyone's advantage here if you are the first to recognise it. The Wall Street crash has shown the red light to the rest of the world, and it will reflect particularly strongly in this country.' He was right of course, and it was a welcome and timely warning.

Apart from my promotion there was something else that compensated for the departure of Sir Malcolm. It concerned 'bags'. During my twelve years in Paper Buildings, I had seldom been able to make any firm social arrangements for my weekday evenings because of having to carry barristers' bags to their homes, when they left chambers. I also had to collect them in the mornings, which meant early rising for me; for that, however, I shall always be grateful, since it was a habit I never lost. At least five times a week I had to take Macnaghten's case to Campden Hill Court, and once or twice a week go to Theo Mathew's house in Gloucester Road. I think perhaps Theo, by staying late, managed to get through most of his work at the office. This procedure added about an hour to my journeys, and over the years, inches to my arms which were always stretched, and at times almost pulled out of their sockets by the sheer weight of the cases. Macnaghten could be a wily old devil; some evenings when his bag was extra heavy, he would say, 'If you find it too weighty for you, Sydney, take out the white book.' This was a particularly thick volume, which he often seemed to want by him. When he'd left chambers I'd open the case to follow his advice, but the book never seemed to be there on these occasions. It was his way, I suppose, of excusing himself, and he knew I wouldn't confront him. Another thing that used to annoy me was that when I collected it I knew that often the bag had never been opened. I proved this from time to time by sticking bits of stamp paper around the sides. I don't know why I troubled, for again, it got me nowhere. I also made no money out of the extra work. It was carefully calculated that my additional fares would cost me a penny for Sir Malcolm, or twopence if I was also taking Mathew's bag. At one time it was the ability to carry 'bags' that was considered to be the first qualification for a junior clerk. That was the reason for their recruitment from the offspring of men servants, mainly footmen's sons. When Sir Malcolm left, the party was over; junior clerks now stipulated that they wouldn't consider any position that entailed bag carrying, and I can't say I blamed them.

Any mention I have made so far to Theobald Mathew has appeared to be slighting; his undistinguished appearance, his late hours, his bag, so that it may come as some surprise when I now say without question, and at the risk of giving offence to some of the great figures that I later met, and whom I served, that Theo was the greatest man I have ever known. I am not alone in this. Listen to this tribute from Sir Patrick Hastings:

If from the many figures that I know so well there is one who stands out among them all, it was one who was known to few people outside his own profession, but loved by everyone in it; a man with a mind that saw humour in everything, and a heart that held sympathy for everyone. I can see him now, strolling through his beloved Temple, where he loved to saunter, perhaps arm in arm with a distinguished judge, commiserating with him upon the stupidity of the Junior Bar, or sympathising with a member of the self-same Bar upon the stupidity of judges. No one was too highly placed to be safe from criticism, no one was too lowly for his friendship and encouragement; many a pompous Silk has been chastened and subdued by his caustic comments; many a quivering junior has been uplifted by his kindly smile. He knew when sorrow was so real that it could be shared in silence; when troubles were so imaginary that they could best be laughed away. Perhaps Theo Mathew did not achieve the great success of others I could name, but then he did not want success; he was a glorious companion and will be remembered long after many of his more famous contemporaries are forgotten.

To me he will remain forever as a living picture of all I have loved best at the Bar.

This was not an obituary notice. It was written in 1949, ten years after Mathew's death, and about a man who was always a junior, for Theo never took Silk and never became a judge. I think it will be as well if I start by giving the bare bones of the man, and try and add the flesh later.

He was born in 1866, the elder son of Lord Justice Mathew, and great nephew of Father Theobald Mathew, the Apostle of Temperance in Ireland. He was educated at the Oratory School, and at Trinity College, Oxford, and was called to the Bar by

48

Lincoln's Inn in 1885. He was a pupil of Joseph Watson, who was then a junior in a large commercial practice and later appointed judge. Theo joined and travelled the South-Eastern Circuit. He kept his interest in the commercial court, and wrote *The Practice of Commercial Cases*. He acquired a substantial Common Law practice in the High Court. It is, however, common opinion that his most successful period began when he joined Lord Robert Cecil and Malcolm Macnaghten at Number 4 Paper Buildings. Sir Malcolm and he appeared in many Canadian appeals before the Judicial Committee, before Canada adopted the principle and practice of legal nationalism, and in later years he became increasingly the leading specialist on libel. He was a fast but careful worker, though towards the end he suffered from failing eyesight. In the framing of his pleadings there was no one superior to him, and he was a master in the strategy of litigation. He excelled as a lawyer, rather than as an advocate; his intellect got in the way of his advocacy, for he couldn't assume an emotion which he was unable totally to accept, yet he was one of the finest after-dinner speakers of his time. He was a fine teacher, he never had less than four pupils, and there was always a long waiting list. I suppose now he is chiefly remembered for his wit as evidenced in his *Forensic Fables* and *For Lawyers and Others*, and in a way, since the drawings and the words are so personal, they are the best indication of the character of the man. They show his unique and delightful sense of the ridiculous, his marked dislike for anything pretentious, and his deep-rooted kindliness. He was a sunny wit, it seemed he basked in the affection in which he knew he was held. Yet in court he never attempted humour. Judicial joking and jesting was a habit he abhorred. He died in June 1939, and the greatness of the company of the judges and lawyers who attended his Requiem Mass was an indication of the love and esteem in which he was held.

That in a nutshell then was Theobald Mathew. It was an image that stayed with me during the twenty-three years that I served him. I had hoped in this chapter to separate the years so that here I would deal with my life until 1928, when I became a chief clerk. I find, though, that I cannot do this as far as my relationship with

Theo is concerned. It is impossible for me to relate it chronologically, it remains all of a piece with me and in that way I shall have later to treat it. There is a theory that good men make poor copy. I hope I can disprove this.

There were three other barristers practising in our chambers of whom I saw nothing during my first three years in Paper Buildings, Hubert Hull, Richard Ludlow and Austin Longland, for they were engaged in the services, or in war work. It wasn't an easy time for any returning young barristers, their names had been forgotten, and solicitors, like many others, were not concerned about making Britain a land fit for heroes to live in.

I particularly remember one case in which Austin Longland was concerned; it happened on circuit at Stafford. It was a matter of personal injury; Norman Birkett was leading for the plaintiff, a lady, and Longland was a junior on the other side, representing an insurance company. The brother of the plaintiff was a very rich man, who had been angered by what he considered the devious and delaying tactics of the company. When he met Birkett he told him that the money meant nothing to him, but that it apparently meant everything to the insurance company, so he wanted him to hit them where it hurt most. 'I don't think they will settle out of court for more than £15,000,' Birkett replied. 'That's not enough, I want £30,000,' came the answer. 'It's that or nothing, and if they refuse you'll fight them to the last ditch, and if in the end you get nothing, I shall not blame you.' Birkett couldn't believe his ears. 'Sir,' he said, 'you are giving me the opportunity of a lifetime. It's an occasion I've always dreamed of. This is the way I see it, they will begin by believing that I'm bluffing, then they will think that perhaps I've got something up my sleeve, and finally they will be so certain that I have, they will not dare to go into court. I must warn you, though, that there is the element of risk; remember, it now becomes a poker game.'

'You've got my instructions, good luck to you,' came the firm reply. It went as Birkett had foretold. I was able to hear the other side of the story from Longland. At first counsel and client were scornful, then apprehensive, then when their 'final offer' of £25,000 was refused, they were in turmoil, they didn't know what to advise. Finally it was Birkett's broad smile that decided the matter; the clients' nerve went, and with a wailing and a gnashing of teeth, they paid a cheque into court. Later still, I heard from Archie Bowker, Birkett's chief clerk, that this was an occasion when counsel got his fee within a week.

So during those years to 1928 I served my time, enjoyed my work and gained a quite considerable experience both of the Law and the qualities of men concerned in it, through those I worked for, and with. They were my formative years you might say. I also had a deal of fun. There was more laughter out of court than in, and Wootton, despite, or perhaps because of, his fondness for the bottle, was an easy and amiable cove to be with. Perhaps I owe him more than I have given him credit for.

Chapter Four

In spite of my long working day I was able to enjoy some social life. During the first two years at the Temple this was confined to visits to the cinemas or music halls with Pop, or walking around with friends that I had made at evening classes; boys who, like myself, were training as clerks. Girls didn't want to know anyone as young or impecunious as I was – I wouldn't have got very far sharing a whipped cream walnut with them on a Saturday. Occasionally I watched Chelsea if I got away on time but usually I managed to see only the last half of the game.

I was seventeen or eighteen when I became aware that girls were beginning to look at me, and show me that I was, as it were, in with a chance. My friends and I took to promenading up and down Putney High Street, or Kings Road, Chelsea, studying the form and flashing our eyes at anything we considered worth our fancy. Now was the time when skirts were starting to get shorter, and we got the same thrill from a bit of leg that our fathers had from peeping at ankles. One day we got into conversation with a group of girls. At first it was a sort of self-conscious giggling session, then I noticed one who took my fancy. I don't remember her real name, but as she announced, 'My friends call me Fluff,' that's how I knew and referred to her. We became very close, though we kept well within the bounds of the code for sweethearts at that time. I felt no end of a dog as we walked together over Putney Heath on a Sunday afternoon, or took our time over a glass of ginger pop in a cafe near the local cinema.

I found I had something in common with the Kaiser, I was

particularly attracted by girls' forearms. I'd read somewhere that he chose the women for his wife's bedchamber for the beauty of their forearm – indeed it may have been that that started me looking at them, and finding that they had the same appeal for me; legs, even bosoms, took second place. Fluff's forearms were perfectly formed, and gave me a deal of satisfaction.

I don't know how Mum got to know that I was walking out, women's instinct I expect, but one day she cornered me and started chatting about it. 'I'd like to see her, Sydney,' she eventually said. Of course it was not possible for me to ask Fluff to tea, that would have been tantamount to saying that we were courting, so it was arranged that I would take her to the cinema, that later Mum would come too, and sit near us, so that when the film was over we could meet 'accidentally' in the foyer, and I could introduce them. Everything went according to plan, but it was a great mistake, for when it came to the introduction and I said, 'Mum, this is Fluff,' I saw her eyes twinkle. I wasn't surprised therefore when I got home to be met with a barrage of banter about 'Sydney and his bit of Fluff'. It wouldn't have been so bad if the joke had been confined to Mum and Pop, but my sister seized on it; she was at that awful in-between age that all girls go through, and she made my life hell by spreading the news amongst our mutual friends. There was only one way out, Fluff had to go. At my age, and at that time, a man's dignity came first.

For a year or so I pursued the policy of non-involvement with the opposite sex. I'd meet girls in a group in our particular cafe society, but I remained fancy free which gave me time to follow in my father's footsteps as an entertainer. Although like him I had perfected a Eugene Stratton act, I now began to study other performers, Bransby Williams, Nelson Keys and my greatest love of them all, the clown Grock. With no modesty at all, I believed then, and I still do now, that my impersonation of Grock was as near perfect an imitation as possible. Pop had worked up a local reputation as a performer at concerts and Masonic evenings, and he introduced me to this world. Much of the entertaining was for charity, but I also managed to earn some extra money. If it hadn't been for the 'bags' I could have earned considerably more.

After the war, dancing became all the rage first among the Flappers and later at our level, too, and I was caught up in the craze. Whenever I did anything, I liked to do it as well as possible, so I took lessons. Socially it paid off. I may only have been five foot five, but I was continually in demand as a partner and my patter seemed to please if ever I was able to sit a dance out, though most of it was second-hand material I'd picked up at the music halls. The combination of these two graces gave me considerable advantage over the muscular local Lotharios.

When the Charleston came in I had some difficulty in learning it. Then I saw an advertisement that announced that a Mr Henry Cooper, who had taught the Prince of Wales, was prepared to give lessons, in a course lasting twelve weeks. Mr Cooper was indeed an excellent instructor, and I thoroughly enjoyed the first session, but it was the first and last as far as Mr Henry was concerned. He was there to take our money, whet our appetites, then leave the rest of the classes to his girls. Still, at the end of it I came away with a fair ability, though I sometimes wondered whether it had been worth the money, for the word got around the Temple of my prowess, and for months afterwards Number 4 Paper Buildings was invaded by clerks of all ages who expected me to instruct them free.

Through my friendship with one of the junior clerks, Arthur Swann who was employed in Singleton KC's chambers, I discovered St Bride's Institute. It was, and I believe still is, an educational and recreation centre in the city and near to the Temple. It was an excellent meeting place; we could eat, swim and dance there, and, if we were so minded, attend a variety of lectures and concerts. Swannee was great East End character, with a quick-fire wit of a Cockney, and the looks of an Ivor Novello.

He had a sister with looks as brilliant as his own; unfortunately she had a voice like gravel, and a strong accent with it. He often brought her to St Bride's with him. He had plans for his sister and me. 'She'd make you a wonderful wife, Syd, like me to fix it for you? She'll do anything I tell 'er. Think what a great set-up it would be, you and me could go out nights together for the rest

54

of our lives.' He may have looked like Ivor Novello, but there the similarity stopped. He had no romance in his make-up. He was a realist was Swannee.

I was still living at home. It was a happy place that I took for granted. Mum and Pop got closer as they grew older, my sister I'm glad to say grew up and we became good friends. Mum continued to run the house with her paying guests, and her cooking still found favour. Pop and his business survived, and he enjoyed his visits to the halls and his occasional 'gigs'. It came as a shock, therefore, when in 1926 Mum found a lump in her breast. She went to the doctor, and then to hospital, where she had the breast removed. Cancer in those days was a dread word; it is of course today, though the operations and treatment are more generally successful. Our guests all had to leave, for after two months away, it was apparent that she would never be able to run that business again. She seemed for a time to recover, and although we were all shaken by what had happened, our hopes began to rise. Then she developed a cough, and it was obvious that the disease had spread to her lungs. She returned to hospital where she lingered, often in great pain, for eighteen months.

It was the end of security for my father, my sister and myself. My sister and I were lucky, we had our work and our friends, and before Mum died I had been able to tell her of my promotion. For Pop it was a disaster, for when Mum went into hospital for a second time, without her restraining influence, he took to the bottle. I couldn't blame him, but he became impossible to live with. My sister continued to try to keep the home going, while I took a room in Frederick Street, near the Temple. I visited home regularly to help to keep the place clean, and to try and make Pop see the error of his ways. Then the crunch came. One evening, just before I was leaving the Temple, my sister phoned to say that she couldn't get into the house. Pop had locked and bolted the doors, and she could see him in the sitting-room, out cold, with a bottle of whisky at his side. I rushed round there, but although we knocked and hammered he wouldn't let us in; he woke but shouted and swore at us, telling us to leave him alone. Eventually we decided that there was nothing for it but to do just that.

We booked in at a small hotel nearby for the night, and were round early the next morning. Still Pop refused to open the door. Today I suppose people would call the police for help, but at that time it was the absolute last resort for respectable folk, the neighbours would find out and our bubble reputation would be burst. I decided to take counsel's opinion. I went to our chambers and waited for Theo Mathew to arrive. Rather shamefacedly I explained the predicament; I needn't have worried, it was the kind of situation that he loved, something that called for strategy, tactics and a plan of action. He summoned Hubert Hull and Hugh O'Donnel, a red-headed retired army major, who had recently joined our chambers. The plan that was drawn up was a simple one. Hull, O'Donnel and I would take the train to Parson's Green Station. There Hull would engage a cab. Explaining something of our purpose to the driver, we would then go to my home, where O'Donnel would lead the assault and break in to the house. We would bundle Pop into the taxi, and drive back to the Temple where Mathew would be waiting to deliver a homily and an ultimatum to him. It was also agreed that I would telephone my sister, and that she would be on the spot to meet us and take possession of the house. There was a dogged sense of purpose about the three of us as we set out to go into battle. Everything went according to plan on the outward journey, though when we arrived there was no sign of my sister. O'Donnel, eyes alight, sprang from the cab, and rapped on our door fiercely. It was opened by my sister, who was waving a piece of paper. We all poured into the sitting-room. There was no evidence of Pop. Then my sister explained that when she had arrived earlier the door was no longer locked. She'd found on the hall table a note which Pop had written, which read, 'I'm sorry about what happened, please forgive me, and come back home. Love, Pop.' It was of course a complete anti-climax, and I think a great disappointment to both my barrister companions, in particular to O'Donnel who was kindled with the fire of battle. It was Hull, though, who broke the silence that Pop's few words has created. 'It's not good enough Sydney, we must now dictate the terms of surrender,' and so saying, he pulled a notebook from his pocket and began writing

56

in it. Eventually I left a note for Pop, telling him that I would see him that evening at home, and that my sister, in the meantime, would stay with some friends. When we met he was indeed most penitent, and agreed to mend his drinking ways and to allow my sister to run the house. He was as good as his word, for with only minor lapses he behaved in as civilized a manner as he was capable of.

When my mother died the home was broken up, my sister moved in permanently with her friends and Pop went into lodgings. He later married a highly respectable woman, who ran a hairdressing establishment. They lived contentedly for a time, but eventually separated. It was the same trouble that he had had with Mum, the histrionics got between them, and he became more of an actor laddie than any of the professionals of the time.

When it had become obvious that Mum was unlikely to recover, I began looking at girls not as dancing companions, but as permanent partners. I suppose I was egged on by my aunts, my mother's sisters, who were frequent visitors to London now that Mum was in hospital. 'It's time you thought about settling down Sydney, and finding yourself a good wife,' was the kind of remark that they bandied around. When they thought that I wasn't responding, I was asked up to Leicester, to meet examples of what they thought would make 'Good wives'. Our opinions didn't tally. Then my aunt Pell, who was married to an army officer and lived in Aldershot, took over. She told me she had found exactly the right girl for me. I went there, and we were introduced. My aunt must have noticed my lack of enthusiasm, for she took me on one side and whispered, 'She's got such a lovely soul, Sydney dear.' I kept my thoughts to myself; lovely soul she might have had, but what a body! This was further emphasised that same night when I took her to a dance; it was like pushing a wheelbarrow around the floor. Her soul didn't seem that highly polished either, for when I took time off, and danced with someone else, she sulked for the rest of the evening.

However, I was brought up in the time when family was family and expected to be kept in touch with events and to be allowed to pass their opinion, so when eventually I thought I had found the right one, I took her to Leicester for inspection. Billie was a super girl, with dazzling good looks; she treated the aunts in copybook fashion and they took her to their hearts. Despite the way she had behaved, Billie didn't take to them, as she told me on the train, when we were returning home. 'I don't like being treated like some prize cow at a cattle show,' she said, 'particularly when I dislike the judges.' I tried soothing her down, and thought I had succeeded but ever afterwards if we had any difference of opinion, it always seemed to come back to the aunts, so in time the affair fizzled out.

The trouble was that Billie's image had stuck in the aunts' minds and so the three other girls that I introduced to them were 'Not a patch on Billie, Sydney dear.' So finally I decided that the decision must be mine and mine alone, that the next time, whenever that might be, I would introduce my lady as 'My bride to be.' I also determined that I would no longer look for a wife, or take 'counsel's opinion,' but would leave it for fate to decide; and I was right.

St Bride's it was that brought me it's namesake. Swannee and I had gone to the institute on our own, and having nothing better to do sat in on a dancing class, studying the form. The pupils were in two lines, and were practising steps as they moved down the hall. When they came near to where we were sitting, I noticed a couple of attractive girls and I nudged Swannee. 'Those two aren't here to learn, they're here to practise.' He cast his professional eye over them, and agreed. At that moment the instructor called out, 'Take partners, please.' Swannee and I rose and walked over to the particular two. I thought I got what in those days was called the 'glad eye' from one of them, so working on the maxim of playing hard to get, I ignored her and took her companion in my arms. Although she was quite a good partner, my mind was on her friend and as we chatted I must have made this obvious, for when the dance came to an end she said in the hearing of both Swannee and her friend, 'If you're so interested in Dora, why don't you talk to her yourself.' I asked Dora to join me in the next dance, and concentrated on trying to re-establish myself through my expert footwork. As I'd thought earlier, she was an excellent dancer and was able to follow even the most intricate steps, so I gained no immediate tactical advantage. We sat a couple of dances out, and now I expected to be able to impress her with my greater experience and sophistication. I was tongue-tied, while she babbled away cheerfully. We spent the rest of the evening dancing. Swannee wasn't enjoying himself, and he told me so. 'It's all right for you, Syd, but there's nothing in it for me.' I was able to placate him, for Do, the abbreviation that everybody called her by, had told me she had a younger sister, Stella. I suggested that if he would hang on for tonight, I would try and arrange for them both to come to a special dance that was being held on the following Saturday.

My invitation was graciously accepted, and when Swannee met Stella he was more than happy with the arrangement. So the four of us went through the next few months. I recovered the use of my tongue and found that I was more and more contemplating a permanent relationship. While I wasn't chancing my arm with my aunts, I became anxious to meet Do's parents. It was a case of the biter being bitten. I was first introduced to her mother, who was manageable. Her father was very different; antagonistic and adamant. 'You're much too old for Do,' he said to me, 'I don't like it, I don't like it at all.' I did everything I could to ingratiate myself, but he had made up his mind. We tried ignoring him, but this made things worse, and eventually he forbade Do to see me. There was no alternative but to accept defeat. Do was under twenty-one and if we had decided to elope, I knew only too well what the consequences would have been.

For weeks I nursed a broken heart. Swannee wasn't sympathetic, for he was deprived of Stella's company. I found, however, that even the most tender of hearts heals with time, and that mine was no exception so I began to look around again.

That Christmas there was a fancy dress dance at St Bride's, a carnival affair which Swannee and I attended with two new partners. Everything was going well, until to my surprise, I saw Do dancing with some young sprig. It upset me, but we studiously ignored each other. The M C then called for a Paul Jones, and when the music stopped, there was Do opposite me. There was nothing else for it, we stumbled into each other's arms and when that particular dance was over Do took my hand and said, 'Let's get away together.' She took me to a nearby cafe; we must have looked an odd couple in our fancy dress. We exchanged our unhappinesses of the past months, and swore eternal love. She told me she'd made her father's life as wretched as possible since we'd parted, and she was sure now that it would be a welcome relief for him that we were together again. I hadn't her confidence, but allowed myself to be persuaded. She was right. Shortly afterwards it was agreed that we could get married. I did then risk taking Do to see the aunts. They were enchanted by her. I didn't however tell anyone in chambers of my plans; they were only informed a few days before when I had to ask for time off for our honeymoon.

The wedding took place at St Andrew's Church, Holborn, on 6 October 1934. Now I'd always thought till then that it was the greatest day in the life of the bride, and to a lesser extent, that of the bridegroom. Pop thought differently. All had gone as I thought it should, until it came to the speeches. He was not included as an official speaker, but he rose to his feet quite steadily and launched into a peroration. Even I must admit that it was gloriously funny. He had the guests in his pocket from the beginning although, as I told him later, there was no need for him to have kept them there and given them encore after encore. It seemed my sister and I were the only two present who resented this take-over, perhaps because we had heard so much of it before, but our efforts to bring down the curtain were in vain. Eventually Do and I crept away to change. When it became obvious that we were about to leave, Pop did at last stop and we were given a good send off. I learned later that it was treated as an interval, so it was cold comfort to be congratulated on our return with remarks like, 'A wonderful wedding, Sydney, pity you missed the best part of it, your dad was just great.' I must say Do was splendid about it. I think secretly she was rather proud of him.

Although I hadn't invited anyone from Paper Buildings to the ceremony they were very generous with their gifts and anxious to hear all about it. I didn't go into detail, however, but just painted the normal beautiful picture. Theo Mathew, I believe, was disappointed not to have been there; he was particularly generous with his present, and kept pressing me for information about Do. Finally I decided that the only thing was to invite her to chambers to meet him. Believing that he was a bit of a woman-hater – it was an impression he went out of his way to give – I warned Do that she might not have an easy passage. When she just smiled and said, 'I shall look forward to it,' I wondered whether I was doing the right thing.

Do duly arrived at Number 4, and I took her into Theo's office and introduced them. I hung around, expecting that the three of us would be in conversation. Theo had other ideas. 'We don't want to keep you from your work Sydney, do we Mrs Aylett?' he said sweetly. 'In any case we have things to discuss which are not for his ears.'

After what seemed an eternity, Do and Theo emerged chuckling together like fellow conspirators and came to my office. 'Thank you, Sydney, for the privilege of meeting your wife. I've learned a lot, and I think in modesty I can say that she has learned a little from me.' Then he turned to Do and said, 'Thank you for coming, Mrs Aylett, I shall look forward to our next meeting, in the meantime, don't let the poor man starve, eh?' That evening Do told me something of what took place. Apparently Theo had begun by adopting the lawyer's attitude, and had submitted her to a cross-examination. She had made a good witness. Then he sprang the question, 'Can you cook?' 'Yes, I think I can say I am quite a good cook,' Do replied. 'What can you cook?' 'Sausages.' 'Sausages! They're not a meal for a hard working man.' 'The way I cook them they are,' said Do gamely. 'How do you cook them?' 'I grill them.' 'I prefer mine fried,' said Theo. 'It's a matter of taste, Sydney prefers his grilled.' 'Mm,' Theo pondered for a moment, then looked for the trick question 'But what do you do before you grill them?' Do was flummoxed. 'Think woman, think, this is vital,' he cried. Still Do remained speechless. 'You puncture them with a fork!' Theo picked up his paper knife, 'Like this,' and he stabbed it on his desk several times. Then they both roared with laughter. Do it was that got the last word. Theo had done his summing up, and had finally sentenced us to a lifetime of happiness. Do thanked him for the kind things he had said. 'I very much hope you are right, Mr Mathew, I only have one doubt.' 'A doubt, Mrs Aylett, already? I don't like the sound of that. A doubt after a matter of weeks with Sydney?' 'Yes,' said Do meekly, 'you see he has a mistress.' 'A mistress!' Theo echoed. 'The scoundrel, but I find it hard to believe.' 'Yes, it's the Temple, he's been living with her for years, and I'm afraid I shall always have to take second place.'

Do and I rented a flat in Victoria. Unlike most married couples at that time we had done our family planning and decided not to have a baby for a couple of years. Despite my innocence I had a certain theoretical experience in such matters, for our chambers had been concerned in the case of Doctor Marie Stopes! It was through a libel action she had brought in 1923 against a Doctor Halliday Sutherland and Harding and More. Theo Mathew was appearing with Sergeant Sullivan KC for the second defendants. After trials in the High Court, the Court of Appeal and the House of Lords, Marie Stopes was eventually defeated but since the case and the notoriety it received served to bring about the social revolution she required it must in another sense have been looked on by her as a triumphant success.

Two years later when I was earning very good money Do decided to buy a house in the country outside London. We found one in Petts Wood, in those days little more than a village. Everything worked out as we had hoped, and to our delight Do became pregnant.

I suppose we should have known better than to accept Pop's offer to buy the pram, but when he made it it seemed a kind and thoughtful gesture. We met him one Saturday morning in a West End shop. Unknown to me Pop had developed a new talent, ventriloquism, and as we wandered around he began practising it. He found a life-size doll decorating one of the prams, lifted it out and carried it round the shop with him. 'What does baby think of this one?' he'd ask, and then launch into baby's opinion. I tried remonstrating with him, but it was no good.

The other customers were delighted with his performance, even the saleswomen joining in the fun. One person was not amused, the floor walker, and he made his presence felt. 'Be quiet, Sir, that kind of mockery is not welcome here,' he bellowed. 'I don't think you realise that having a baby is a very serious business.' That started Pop off on another track. 'It is indeed, Sir,' he said, with his eyes on the floor walker's midriff, 'as it appears you should well know. Come along children, this is no place for our baby,' and he led the way out of the shop, screaming like a newborn infant. In the end we agreed that we would choose the pram ourselves, and send the bill to Pop.

On 13 March 1936 Carol-Anne was born, and as the months passed she made it plain that she had inherited her grandfather's talent. She too was completely uninhibited, and it was therefore inevitable that eventually she would become an actress.

Chapter Five

I would like to say that Theobald Mathew and I hit it off immediately; we didn't, he wasn't that sort of man. Ours was a relationship that developed as we worked together, into first a kind of mutual respect and trust, then friendshop, which finally, as far as I was concerned, developed into love, and I use the word unashamedly. The artist Sir William Orpen had caught the likeness and inner character of Theo in a few minutes after dinner; he had made a sketch on the back of a menu. I saw it daily, for it hung framed in his room, and I was constantly astonished at what it revealed of the man as I knew him; the thinning, untidy hair, the bushy eyebrows, the pince-nez spectacles, which seemed to accentuate his turned-up nose, the half-closed eyes, as if he was in a state of permanent concentration and the delicate hands, which I watched in court and in chambers, wickedly sketching and caricaturing judges, counsel, juries and witnesses.

He was very much a family man, he had nine children, six sons and three daughters, but although they were the cause of great pleasure he worried about them, often I thought unnecessarily, for with the exception of one son, who was severely shell-shocked in the First World War, and through no fault of his own had severe behavioural problems, they were a gifted and loving family. It was his daughters who gave him most concern. He was fond of women, but I don't think he found it easy to understand them, so he gave up and, as I've said earlier, pretended to be a woman-hater. It was a thin mask, for I have seen clever and attractive ladies twist him round their fingers. Perhaps he felt that at home he did not get the respect that he merited, after all there is some truth in the saying that behind every success-ful man, there is an astonished wife, and this of course might have been taken to include his daughters. He was constantly complain-ing about their untidiness. Eventually he told me, with great glee, how he had been able to cure them of the habit. Every so often his local Catholic church would have a jumble sale; a priest, Father Bands, was the organizer, and he would call on his parishioners, wheeling a barrow, to collect unwanted bits and pieces. Theo laid a plot; he invited the father to visit when all his womenfolk were out, showed him up to his daughters' rooms, and told him he could have whatever he found lying around. The good man took him at his word. Later when Theo was confronted with the baleful cries of his daughters he said coolly, 'The careless way you had left your things made Father Bands think that you had no further use for them. If you still want them you will have to go to the jumble sale and buy them back. It should be of some consolation to you that your money will go to an excellent cause.' Apparently the trick worked, for if ever after that their rooms showed a hint of untidiness, he would threaten them with 'Father Bands'.

Theo was regularly hoist with his own petard. Nuns with their collecting boxes were constant visitors to Number 4. They had no conscience about which faith they took money from, but in particular they seemed to enjoy teasing as much as they could from him. It was all a great game in which everyone took part. I would usher them into his room. He would stand up, throw his hands in the air and stamp his feet. 'I've told you, Sydney, never to allow these women into our chambers again, they are rogues and thieves. They come in here in God's name, and then rob the poor.' The sisters would stand there beaming. Theo would point at them, 'Look, Sydney, they laugh me to scorn,' then he would fall into his seat, put his head into his hands, and with resigna-tion say, 'Come on in, sit down and say a prayer for my im-mortal soul, but I shan't give you a single penny for doing it.' I would then withdraw, but from my room I could hear them giggling and chuckling together. Then after about ten minutes they would emerge with the nuns still beaming, and as they went down the corridor Theo would stand shaking his fist at them. 'You're wolves in sheep's clothing,' he would shout, most inaptly. 'Never darken my doors again.' It was the kind of play acting he revelled in.

He pretended to deplore the admission of women to the Bar, yet eventually he took them as pupils, enjoyed having them and using them as flintstone to his wit. The first one, I remember, was a delightful young lady called Miss Monica Geikie Cobb. She was a tall, well-built girl. Theo used her as a model in one of his *Forensic Fables*. It was where a judge who, knowing that there was a woman barrister appearing before him for the first time, decided that he would treat her kindly. But because of her size and manner and wig, he mistook her for the blue-eyed young barrister on the other side, dealt gently with him, and gave her a very hard time of it.

An occasion typical of Theo's attitude towards his lady pupils was the day when he came into chambers and directed me to find two of them. 'I've discovered a use for you at last,' he cried, when we returned. 'This afternoon we are to receive a visit from members of the Bar Association of the United States of America, and they have asked for a conducted tour of the Temple and the Royal Courts of Justice. You have been selected as guides. Now go away, study your history, and report back here at two o'clock.' They did as they were told. After the tour was over Theo asked them how they had got on. 'Splendidly,' answered one of the girls. 'They all seemed most enthusiastic, in fact I would say they were quite bowled over by it all.' The other girl, Miss Caruthers, remained silent, though it was obvious to me that she had her tongue in her cheek. 'And what about you, my dear?' asked Theo, 'How did you get on?' 'Well,' she replied, 'I think it was me that was slightly bowled over.' 'And what do you mean by that?' 'Everything was going fine until the end. Then one of the visitors took my hand in his.' 'The villain,' thundered Theo. 'Well go on, what happened next?' 'Then he pressed it, rather hard.' 'Pressed it!' Theo echoed, in the style of Lady Bracknell. 'What did you do?' 'Eventually I was able to take it

away, but there was something stuck in the palm of my hand.'
'Good heavens, what was it?' 'A sixpence,' said the young lady,
smiling as she held it up between thumb and forefinger for us to
see. Theo pretended not to be amused. 'It's an outrage and an
insult. You're worth much more than that, he should have given
you at least a shilling!'

During his lifetime Theo had many pupils. It is a rule that
anyone who intends to practise at the Bar must read as a pupil,
for a period of at least twelve months, in the chambers of a
practising barrister of not less than five years' standing. It is
possible to do this either before or after being called, or in a split
period. In this time the pupil has the opportunity of seeing, and
occasionally doing, some of the preliminary work, the devilling,
the writing of Pleadings or Opinions, or of learning advocacy by
watching the trials. During his second six months he may accept
instructions and appear in court. The choice of the right master is
therefore of great importance, for a good start is often worth more
than intellect or learning. Apparently I must have voiced this
opinion to Kenneth Diplock, at present one of our Law Lords,
for he told me that when he first came as a pupil to our chambers
and mentioned some high academic qualification, I replied,
'You'd better keep dark about that, otherwise clients will think
you're just a theoretical lawyer.' When I asked Lord Diplock
what he thought of Theo as a teacher, he described him more as a
presence, someone who gave confidence through his learning and
his wit. 'He needed to be bullied to get the most out of him, and
since I was ambitious, I did this and learnt a lot.' Judge Leonard,
another pupil, felt that he taught by just talking.

But how does one judge a good teacher? Today we're told that
we shouldn't go by results. To me this is balderdash. How else in
life are we to be measured? Theo was, like Lord Robert Cecil, a
pupil of Joseph Walton, later a High Court judge. Lord Robert's
summing up of Walton as, 'A man of great personal charm, an
excellent sense of humour, with a faculty for seizing upon the
essential point of any case submitted to him' might easily be
applied to Theo Mathew. Among his pupils were Lord Attlee, the
Socialist Prime Minister, Kingsly Griffith (formerly Chairman of

the Liberal party), Lord Hailsham, one-time Lord Chancellor, Lord Thorneycroft and Sir Stafford Cripps, both one-time Chancellors of the Exchequer, and, as I've already said, Lord Diplock and Judge Leonard to name the few that reached some of the highest offices in the land. The list of distinguished members of the Bar would be a long one. At a dinner given to Theo by his pupils just before his death, 112 attended, which I think gives an indication of the esteem and affection in which he was held.

The pupil room was at Number 1, King's Bench Walk, and nicknamed 'The dog hole.' It had been rightly christened, since it most certainly would never have passed the regulations laid down by the Ministry of Education. In the mornings the pupils would be given Pleadings and Opinions to write, then they would follow Theo over to the Courts, where they would listen to counsel in action, and in the evening at five o'clock they would present their earlier work to Theo, who would 'Point out the dreadful errors of their ways.'

Although there is little that distinguishes one barrister's room from another, Theo did, to some extent, implant his own personality on his. It overlooked the Temple gardens, and it was thought by many to be the most charming and personal in the Temple. It was painted in a deep matt green, and made cosy with its red velvet curtains and large armchair. A familiar winter sight was Theo sitting in this chair, drawn up by the fire and puffing away with a pair of bellows. He didn't like any one else 'messing about with the fire.' and though when he was in court it was often necessary for me, and later my junior, to make it up, it would be quickly unmade when he returned. Sometimes I would hear him chatting away to it. 'The fools don't know how to treat you, do they?' or, 'Now come along, add a little bit of brightness to our lives,' were the sort of remarks he made. There were three Holbein prints on the wall of Sir Thomas More and his family. More was his hero, and particular saint. Theo was a member of the Thomas More Society. He was also a great admirer of Doctor Johnson. There was another picture by Paul Renard, and of course the sketch of himself by William Orpen. On the mantlepiece there was a blue china tobacco jar, and a large casket by the fireplace in which he kept his private papers. The only ornament was a little old man with bow legs, which he looked on as his lucky charm.

I've mentioned Theo's kindness; that, allied to his courtesy, was one of his great characteristics. He had little time for pomposity, overweening conceit, arrogance or selfishness, but I think, because he was able to ridicule these qualities in his sketches, he was able to tolerate people who had them. He was the only man I worked with in the Temple who was able to suffer fools kindly. He hated giving hurt. I remember one day he went out for coffee with Ludlow; they were joined at their table by a solicitor called McKenzie who proceeded to take over the conversation and bore them to distraction. When they left Theo, thinking that McKenzie at least had had the courtesy to stay behind and pay the bill, and believing that he was talking to Ludlow, said, 'What a frightful bore that fellow is. What did you say his name was, McKenzie or something?' 'That's right, Mr Mathew, my name is McKenzie,' came from his side. 'I'm sorry to have spoilt your morning,' and he walked away. Any other man would have taken the situation philosophically, but not Theo; he came back to the chambers almost stricken with grief. 'I've wounded the poor fellow, I wouldn't have done it for the world. What on earth can I do to put it right?' He was eventually persuaded to leave well alone, but it worried him for days.

He couldn't resist an occasional barbed story; there was a particular thick-lipped barrister, who when pronouncing his consonants would shower the court. Theo christened him, 'spit in the eye', and it stuck. One evening there had been a small fire in someone's chambers and the following day Theo was telling a colleague about it. 'The fire brigade must have soon got it under control then,' said his friend. 'Oh they didn't have to call the brigade, they just sent for old "spit in the eye", and he had a word or two with it,' replied Theo.

Another occasion which Ludlow related to me was when they met in a common room of one of the Inns of Court. A number of coloured barristers had assembled there, and when Theo saw Ludlow he went up to him with his arm outstretched, shook him

69

by the hand and said, 'Doctor Livingstone, I presume!'

Only once did Theo wound me; it was partly my fault, I'd chosen the wrong moment. I'd been working at Number 4 for eight years. I'd had one or two small rises in salary, but was only earning twenty-eight shillings a week. I thought I was entitled to another four shillings so I put my case to Wootton who agreed, and passed my request on to Theo. Not only was it turned down, but he added, 'If he wants more money, he must look for a job elsewhere.' It hurt me cruelly. A few days later I discovered that one of his sons had been in financial trouble and had, on that particular day, asked his father to get him out of it. I never repeated my request, and I was earning the same money until my promotion to chief clerk.

Yet Theo could be ridiculously generous at times. He shared my love of the theatre, and we often discussed the shows we'd seen, though in one way our views differed: I saw them from the gallery and sometimes the pit, while he watched from the stalls. Many times when he'd been to a play, he'd say, 'You must go and see it, Sydney,' and a day or so later he would thrust a couple of tickets in my hand. 'There you are, you go, and then we can talk about it together.' They were always the best seats, the equivalent of a week's wages.

He was also fond of films. Claudette Colbert was his favourite star, and Maurice Chevalier was his favourite performer. He had a superstition which linked work with the movies. If ever he looked as though he was going through a slack period, he would leave his room at about two, and without stopping to say where he was going would shout, 'I'm off.' The moment he left, either the phone would start ringing, a solicitor's clerk would be asking for him urgently, or a messenger would arrive with a brief, demanding an immediate opinion. When he returned some three or four hours later, either Wootton or I would say, 'Where on earth have you been, Sir? Everyone's been trying to get hold of you.' Then he would throw his arms into the air and cry, 'It's worked once again. It's worked! I leave the office for only a few solitary hours at the cinema, and everyone realizes how much they need me.'

70

When it came to his own money Theo was philosophical, yet practical. 'Don't demean yourself by arguing with bad solicitors,' he would say to me, 'either they will pay, or they won't.' He wasn't quite right of course; often I was able to force payment out of the most obdurate, and I enjoyed doing it. In fact, Theo had few bad debts, largely because his clients were the big men who wanted to come back to us. But even with them it wasn't always a golden rule; occasionally I would have to say when they came along with a new brief, 'I'm afraid I can't accept this. You owe Mr Mathew £1000 and until that is paid in whole or part, he has told me that he will not accept any more work from you.' He hadn't, of course, but they generally came through with a cheque. As I've said, Theo was a junior and remained one all his life, but when it is considered that he mostly worked for the great leaders of the time, like Birkett, Hastings and Bevan, and received the equivalent of two thirds of their fees, he was probably earning nearly as much as they were, for he would appear more often. If Pat Hastings, for example, was getting 500 guineas for his brief, Theo would get 333 guineas. For a refresher, that is, a fee for every day after the first that he appeared in court, Pat would get 300 guineas, and Theo two hundred, but after the case was over, Pat might not be appearing for another week, whereas Theo was almost constantly busy. When people wonder why he didn't apply for Silk, or why preferment was never offered to him, they forget that it wouldn't have paid him to become a KC, or to accept elevation to the Bench, and that as a family man, one with nine children, he put their well-being first. The payment of juniors came under scrutiny shortly after the Second World War, and some clients wanted to do without them. Pat Hastings quickly quashed this by saying, 'If you're not going to provide a junior, then I want the money you would have paid him as well as my own fee.'

Many people must have wondered how it is that in certain notorious cases, the defendants, who apparently had little money, were able to employ such learned and expensive counsels. The answer is simple; they were paid by newspapers, in return for a full and explicit confession if the defendants were found guilty, or their life story if they were proved innocent. Counsel were only too pleased to accept these assignments, for they kept them in the public eye, were the nearest they could come to advertising, and of course they were certain of their money, win or lose.

Theo was not the only brilliant man to remain a junior, though perhaps he was alone in retaining his place against all the up-and-coming opposition. Indeed, it is common knowledge that he was offered more work during the year before his death than he could cope with. There was another in the Temple at this time who kept himself to the front by more devious methods. He was a specialist in Divorce law and was doing very nicely, but he knew that there were two others whose opinions were valued more than his own, and that he could never overtake them. Short of murder there was only one way. He put it around that he had applied for Silk, and that he'd been advised to do so on the highest authority. He saw to it that word of this got to his two adversaries, whose vanity was predictably offended. They both felt bound to apply themselves. At the last minute our cunning barrister 'withdrew' his application; his competitors were successful, thus leaving him at the head of the field. Attainment is not always achieved by ability alone.

I've mentioned Theo's gift as an after-dinner speaker; unfortunately I was never a witness to it, though I was given many subsequent reports. Sometimes I would stay behind in chambers and help him change, fasten his tie or give him a final brush. I hoped in exchange he would give me some pearl of a story he was going to use, but he never did. I think perhaps he wasn't sure of exactly what he was going to say. One evening I recall there was pandemonium. He was speaking at a dinner where King George V was to be the guest of honour. It was, he considered, part of his wife's or one of his daughter's duties to pack his clothes into a case. To his horror he found that on this occasion the studs of his starched front had been omitted. It allowed him the opportunity of expressing his fury of, and contempt for, the female sex. When his diatribe was over, he panicked slightly. 'What on earth am I going to do, Sydney, I can't present His Majesty with a gaping front.' Frankly I was at a loss as to what to advise. The shops were closed and, although there might have been men in the Temple with a set of studs in their chambers, they would have gone home. Suddenly Theo brightened. 'Have we any paper fasteners, Sydney?' he asked. We had, and I sorted a few out. 'Polish the tops with something,' he demanded, and then fitted them into his shirt. They not only filled the bill, they looked almost opulent. The following day I asked him how he had got on. 'They passed muster,' he replied. 'It wasn't entirely a bloodless victory. I've several scratches to show for my loyalty.' Then he added meaningfully, 'But I've asked Father Bands to call. That should be some consolation for my wounds.'

'These books will last when most of the law books of our generation are forgotten,' a critic wrote of *Forensic Fables*, when they were first published. He was right, they have, and most of the sketches and comments that go with them are as apt today as they were at the time. They are a lasting example of Theo's wit, his dislike for anything pretentious, and his deep-rooted kindliness; without in any way lessening his deep respect for the traditions of his profession, or those who practised it. To me they were, and still are, magic. I had fancied myself as an amateur cartoonist before I saw Theo's work, but I seldom put pen to paper afterwards. I was lucky to be in from the beginning of their creation, but I had missed his first sketches which were published in the *Westminster Gazette*, on or about the year 1910. These were a series of caricatures uncomplimentary to the peerage, called 'The Story of an Ancient Line', and 'The Press and the Budget. Why Some of Them Voted Against it.' They were in the Liberal interest and were described as 'the cleverest caricatures the campaign has produced.'

Forensic Fables first appeared as single, regular contributions to the *Law Journal*, then Butterworth suggested to him that they publish them as a book. Such was their success that book followed book. It was like some star performer; a final performance, a further final performance, and the positively last final performance. In a later reprint David, one of Theo's sons, says that they were composed in his father's study at 31 Cornwall Gardens. No doubt many were, but others, as I can bear witness, saw the light of day in Paper Buildings. From time to time I would be called into his room to model for him, the most uncomfortable occasion being when I had to fall over in front of his fire and and hold my right leg in the air. His pupils were similarly employed. Often he used the Royal Courts of Justice as a studio. I've seen judges who, catching him sketching out of the corner of their eyes, would preen themselves, and take up a position, which showed that to appear in a fable was regarded by even the most lofty as a privilege and a mark of their distinction. His family also modelled for him, in particular his girls, and I think 'The wiles of his women', a phrase that was often on his lips, provided some of the material, for his work did not always concern points of law or courtroom behaviour, or misbehaviour.

One of the fables I enjoy most was about Little Effie, a ward of court. The case was concerned with whether she should be educated privately or be sent to school. The kindly judge, as judges did then and indeed do now, decided to entertain Effie in his chambers, to determine the character of the child. He liked her, and was attracted by her cropped hair and large blue eyes. To put her completely at her ease he invited her to try on his wig, and later to observe the effects in a looking-glass. He then put his wig back on and returned to court. The counsel resumed his case. 'A month ago,' he said, reading the mother's affidavit, 'Effie suffered from a bad attack of ring worm and her head had to be shaved.' The judge immediately adjourned the proceedings (*sine die*), and sent his clerk out for a bottle of Condy's fluid.

Another favourite of mine concerned a laundress in the Temple, and to her huge delight Mrs Hayden, our laundress, was selected as a model. She didn't raise any objections later when she discovered that in the fable she was called Sarah Stout. Theo was a great one for the exaggerated stomachs (he put them on me) in all shapes and sizes. Although *Forensic Fables* was the work of a few years there was at one time in our chambers a pile of notebooks with, opposite the notes of evidence, sketches covering thirty years and which included caricatures of every judge, Silk and junior in practice during that time. It was a great tragedy that it eventually was my job to see that these were not handed down for posterity.

74

Some colleagues of Theo's suggested to him that it might cause hurt, either to the people concerned or to their children, if the drawings were to be published after his death. This so worried him that he gave me instructions to burn his books, and to continue to do the same after every future case. It was, as I've said, painful for me at the time, and since has assumed even greater proportions. After he died, we sorted through his papers and to our delight we found his original working copy of one book of *Forensic Fables*. Unfortunately someone allowed one of the pupils to borrow it. He later said that he had lost it; that he had left it in a tea shop. A likely story!

As a lawyer Theo's brilliance was as a strategist rather than as an advocate. His Opinions and Pleadings, which are the basis of any action, were supreme. Only once did I hear them seriously questioned, and that strangely enough was by Sir Patrick Hastings, his great friend and colleague. One day as they were about to go into court Pat rounded on Theo and said, 'You haven't justified this case, we should be pleading completely differently. Now there isn't time to change, and my hands are tied. I can't see how I'm going to pull it out of the fire.' Theo remained calm, and throughout the case advised Pat and the Action was won. Nor did he take up the cudgels afterwards, he simply said, 'In future I will not plead a case for Pat without a prior consultation.' And he never did.

Another thing that is perhaps not generally known is that nineteen out of twenty cases never come to trial, they are either dropped or settled out of court, and it was on those nineteen that Theo's skills were most in evidence. One day a titled young lady came to see him with her solicitor. She straight away admitted that she had been to several other solicitors about the situation in which she now found herself, that they had asked for counsel's opinion and that their reply had been that she had no claim in Law, since she had acted for immoral considerations. The facts were these; she had contracted with an elderly man to live with him as his mistress, and to act as housekeeper and hostess for a year in return for £10,000, which was to be paid at the end of that time. When the year was over, she asked for her money, and the ungallant fellow told her to go and whistle for it. Theo listened carefully to her story, cross-questioned her and was eventually convinced that she was speaking the truth. He then told her not to worry, and that he would be able to form a statement of claim. He scribbled on the back of an old envelope for a minute or two and then said, 'We will put in a claim for services rendered. Not, I may say, the immoral services, but those of housekeeper and hostess; for your ability of attracting guests, for business and social purposes, and for advancing his position in society.'

The opposition was particularly strong, Norman Birkett leading Valentine Holmes, both skilled in cases of this kind. Henry Maddox was leading for us, and the case was to be tried by Mr Justice Amery. Before the case came to court Norman Birkett made several offers, which were turned down, and it wasn't until the last minute that he agreed to settle for the original sum asked. Birkett could see that the jury's sympathy must be with the lady; they would know that there was more to it than the role of hostess, and they would brand the fellow a cad and find against him. He congratulated Theo afterwards on what he said was a brilliant Pleading, and followed this with, 'You know, Theo, I have found that cases are like troubles, "They come not single spies, but in battalions". I have four similar ladies who were interested in the outcome of this case. I told them to wait and see what happened, now I shall be able to advise them to go forward.' Theo replied that he didn't think that such a line of argument should apply in every case, 'I wouldn't have advised it if I hadn't been certain that the lady was telling the truth.' He was not always a stickler for the truth. Macnaghten and he once had a ding-dong battle as to whether a lie was ever excusable. Macnaghten was adamant that under no circumstances could it be. 'Right,' said Theo, playing what he thought was his ace. 'What would you say if a homicidal maniac, brandishing a knife, broke into this office and demanded to know the whereabouts of Wootton, who was hiding behind your desk?' Macnaghten, without pausing for a second said, 'That is simple. My reply would be, "It is a question I am not prepared to answer."'

Theo could twist the truth, and used the Law's Delay. This was noticeable in the strategy he used to keep a case out of court and prevent a company from going bankrupt. He was approached by a group of financiers, who had had constructed a large place of recreation and entertainment. When it was completed they found they had insufficient funds to pay the contractors, who started proceedings to get their money. Once again the solicitors had been elsewhere for Opinions, which had been the same, 'pay up or go bust'. Theo had other ideas when he was told that all that was needed was time. He was assured by the clients that their bookings for the first year would more than cover the sum they owed, and that one year was the time that was necessary to fulfil their obligations. In a nutshell Theo's plan was this, 'First get your architect to go over the whole building with a fine tooth comb, looking for faults in construction, equipment and furnishings, no matter how minor these might be. Submit these to the contractors one by one; this should delay any possible proceedings for some considerable time.' They did as he suggested. Eventually the case was entered in the lists, but before it came to court Theo was able to get a postponement. When it came up again, he asked for the case to be transferred to the Official Referee's list, on the grounds that the construction details were varied and complex and would waste the time of the court. The judge readily agreed, so once again the case was put back, and since there was a long list of lengthy cases needing settlement by the Official Referee, Theo was able to gain many months' grace. This was enough for his clients, and so before the time was up he was able to go to the other side, and to settle.

Although Theo was an excitable man, his wrath generally had an assumed theatrical quality. I rarely saw him really angry. He fired, however, with all guns on one firm of solicitors, and sank them and their client without trace. It was not a particularly savoury case. A gentleman with homosexual tendencies had been able to protect himself from prosecution by enlisting the aid of a police superintendent. He rewarded the officer on his retirement by giving him a small annual pension. When the superintendent died he stopped the payment. To his astonishment and concern, he received a letter from the man's son saying that he had been given to understand by his father that the pension would be passed on to him as his heir, and that unless the money was paid he would take the matter to court. The gentleman went to his solicitors, who told him to ignore the matter for the time being. Then the son went to his solicitors who wrote demanding the money. The gentleman, for peace and quiet, was all for continuing the payment, but he was persuaded to take counsel's advice. Theo was very angry. He asked that the son and his solicitors come and see him. 'Do you believe your client's story?' he thundered at the man's advisers. 'Don't you see it as I do as a cloak for blackmail?' The lawyers protested and blustered. 'Very well,' said Theo. 'Now let me tell you what I shall do if you continue with this case. I shall have you before the Law Society, and ask to have you struck off. And you, Sir,' he cried, pointing at the son, 'I will have you in the box at the Old Bailey, and sentenced for the most despicable crime of blackmail. Now get out, don't trouble to think it over, for I mean every word I say.' They were indeed the last words that I, or anyone else, heard of the matter.

The case that perhaps best illustrates Theo's strategic ability concerns that great Liberal leader, Mr Gladstone. It was fortunate that Theo should have been approached, since Gladstone was one of his heroes and he was therefore the most likely lawyer to do everything in his power to safeguard his reputation. The story began in 1926, when the great man's sons. Viscount Gladstone and Mr Henry Gladstone, called at Number 4 with Mr Richard Butler, of Charles Russel & Co., a leading firm of London solicitors. In conference they told Theo that a book had been written by a Captain Peter Wright called *Portraits and Criticisms*, which contained a libellous attack on their father, who had been dead for thirty years. It stated that at the time when Gladstone was believed to have been trying to rescue prostitutes from the evils of their profession, he was in fact consorting with them. The inference therefore was that Gladstone, a fervent churchman, and four times prime minister when Britain was at its height of its glory, was a debauched hypocrite.

Now, judged on today's terms, there could be no doubt that Gladstone acted foolishly and laid himself open to speculative

78

criticism, but in Victorian times do-gooders went in for a deal more personal involvement than they do now, so that his venturing out onto the streets, or occasionally into prostitutes' rooms to talk to them about their spiritual jeopardy, and moral degradation, would not then have seemed so extraordinary, particularly since he had the support and encouragement of his wife, and of a society for the rehabilitation of fallen women.

The Gladstone brothers wanted their father's name cleared. The difficulty was how to do it. English law does not allow the issue of a writ for libel to clear the name of a dead man, and what the brothers wanted was just that kind of an action, where Captain Wright would be in the box and put through the most searching cross-examination, which would lead to the vindication of their father's name. The plan to achieve this, which Theo drew up, was followed. Lord Gladstone wrote an abusive and offensive letter to Captain Wright, calling him a fool, a liar and a coward. Captain Wright replied in equal terms on Bath Club notepaper, a club of which Lord Gladstone was also a member. Theo then suggested that his letter, together with a copy of the foul accusation made against his father, be sent to the secretary of the Bath Club for consideration by the club committee. As a result Wright was expelled from the club by the committee who, fortunately as things turned out, ignored a rule of the club by not inviting the captain to be present at the hearing to give his side of the story. So Wright sued the Bath Club in the High Court, for injury to his character, and the loss of the club's amenities, and was given judgement and awarded damages. Flushed with this success, the captain then decided to continue, and issued a libel writ against Lord Gladstone. This was exactly what Theo had foreseen, and he advised Russel & Co. to plead justification. This meant that if the allegation Lord Gladstone had made against Captain Wright proved to be true, the father's name would be cleared. They would also have the pleasure of having Wright in the box, and they knew that, because of the nature of the case, it would be widely reported so that there would be few who would not know of Gladstone's innocence.

The trial opened on 17 January 1927 before Mr Justice Avory.

Mr Norman Birkett led for us and he was to use the tactics which were based on Theo's strategy. Though the courtroom was crowded and there were many distinguished people present, somehow the ghost of the great Mr Gladstone seemed to hover over us all.

Captain Wright seemed self-assured and composed. He was forty-six years of age, of medium height, with sharp features and well-groomed greying hair. He was, as his counsel told us, a man of good education; an old Harrovian and a graduate of Balliol. He had an excellent war record, and was at one time interpreter and joint secretary to the Executive Committee of the Supreme War Council. Fortunately for us his manner in the witness box denied these advantages. He was over-confident and bombastic, both of which qualities were bound to irritate Mr Justice Avory, who at one time reprimanded him for banging on the witness box to accentuate his argument. Birkett was at his best, and cross-examined him with effortless skill, wringing from the captain admission after admission, that his accusations against Gladstone were all based on hearsay. The knife went in further and further and eventually Birkett, having asked why the captain had not made deeper research into his subject received the astonishing reply, 'I should never be able to write anything if I did.' When it came to that part of the book which stated that Lillie Langtry had been Gladstone's mistress, it again was found to be based on nothing but rumour. Miss Langtry apparently had not previously known of this accusation, and the following day Birkett was able to read a telegram in court in which she strongly repudiated the slanderous allegations. A later implication by Wright that Gladstone had been seduced by a Russian spy, produced the loudest laughter in court. Even lawyers who rarely appear to be confident about a verdict were certain that it would go against the captain. They were right; the jury were out for two and a half hours, and not only found for us but added a rider which said, 'The jury wish to add that in their unanimous opinion the evidence that had been placed before them has completely vindicated the high moral character of the late Mr W. E. Gladstone.' It must have been a debilitating experience for the wretched captain, for he came out of it dishonoured and with a bill for £5000 for costs. The Wright v. Gladstone case will probably go down in legal history as a triumph for Norman Birkett. While not denying the important part he played, there can be no doubt that had it not been for Theo Mathew's plan, it would never have come to court, and the stain on Gladstone's character would be there today.

A case which I know was near to Theo's heart was one which should never have gone to court. It was an example of how costly loss of temper, conceit, vanity and a lack of humour can be. The story behind it was this. A game was invented in 1932, which became very popular with children; indeed it was also played by many adults. It was called Yo-Yo, and versions of it are still being sold today. The owners of the rights in it tried to increase its popularity by advertisement, and commissioned a Mr McNully to prepare the copy. Mr McNully had a young daughter, whose reading had included the *Bab Ballads* and who had been so attracted by the name of Mr Blennerhasset who appeared in them, that she had taken to calling her father by this name on certain occasions. She would wake him in the morning saying, 'It is half past seven, Mr Blennerhasset,' and continue with, 'Will Mr Blennerhasset require a cup of tea?' So when Mr McNully was looking for a name for his advertisement, he decided on what he thought was a mythical Mr Blennerhasset. As it turned out, there was a real Blennerhasset, who was a prosperous and highly respected member of the London Stock Exchange. He was also pompous, so that when the advertisement appeared in May 1932, the younger members of the Stock Exchange, noted for their ready wit, and most probably grateful for the opportunity of visiting it on Mr Blennerhasset, teased him incessantly and he became an object of ridicule, even among some of his friends. While it was probably most unpleasant for the man, he should have realised that in time the merriment would die down and the joke would stale. He didn't; he lost his temper, called on his solicitor and demanded retribution. Perhaps his lawyers advised against his going forward with the action, and he refused to accept their decision; if not he was very badly served by them, for from being a figure of fun in the close confines of the Stock

Exchange, he became the laughing stock of the whole country. The advertisement was a warning:

'Beware of Yo-Yo'

Take warning by the fate of Mr Blennerhasset, as worthy a citizen as any that ate lobster at Pimms', or holed a putt at Walton Heath. 'Sound man Blennerhasset,' they said in Throgmorton Street, and 'Nice people, the Blennerhassets,' was the verdict over the teacups and in the local tennis clubs.

But Yo-Yo got him and now . . . one day Blennerhasset brought his offspring to buy them two nice books, entertaining but instructive. Near the book department they first saw the Yo-Yo being played . . . Blennerhasset, ever responsive to the 'Gimmes' of his young, bought the children one each. At home that evening, with that deprecatory condescension so familiar in parents, he offered to give them the first lesson. Strangely enough the Yo-Yo was recalcitrant. It sulked. First it would and then it wouldn't. But the Blennerhasset blood was up. The dinner gong rang and cried out, but Blennerhasset kept on.

He was determined to make that little devil on a string do its stuff. The nurse took the children to bed, Mrs B. took herself to bed. But Mr Blennerhasset toiled on at Yo-Yo. Came the dawn and he was still there dishevelled and wild-eyed with the Yo-Yo string still dangling from his trembling fingers. They tried to part him from it, but it was no use; and eventually poor Blennerhasset was taken away.

Today he is happy in a quiet place in the country and under sympathetic surveillance he practises Yo-Yo tricks. His old friends at Pimms' miss him at lunch, and three-quarters of a certain foursome have had to find a stranger to make up their quorum.

So beware of Yo-Yo which starts as a hobby and ends as a habit.

There followed a series of pictures showing the disintegration of the unfortunate Mr Blennerhasset.

Now apart from his somewhat unusual name, and the fact that

The author aged 3 with his mother, Lucy, and his sister, Elsie, in 1904.

The author in 1939.

The author on his wedding day, 6th October 1934.

View of the Inner Temple in the 1920s from King's Bench Walk. Paper Buildings are on the extreme left.

F. E. Smith (subsequently Lord Birkenhead).

Lord Robert Cecil.

with love
William Orpen

Pencil drawing of Theobald Mathew by Sir William Orpen.

THE JUDGE OF ASSIZE AND THE
OLD SCHOOL FRIEND

*Cartoons by Theobald Mathew from FORENSIC
FABLES first selected and published in 1949.*

THE ZEALOUS CLERK WHO OVERDID IT

Left *The Right Hon. Lord Diplock.*

Below left *Mr. Justice Macnaghten.*

Below right *His Honour Judge Ifor Lloyd.*

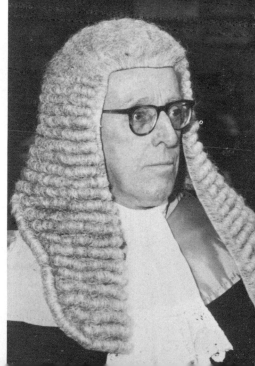

The Right Hon. Lord Hailsham of
St. Marylebone, C.H.

Mr. Justice Maurice Drake.

occasionally he had been to lunch at Pimms', there was no other similarity between the individual, the cartoon and the copy. Patrick Hastings and Theo appeared for us. Again it was a case that attracted a large crowd to the Royal Courts of Justice, and with customary dignity Mr Justice Banson was ushered in to preside over the case. Once it was started the police and the attendants were hard put to it to keep a decent silence. Several young members of the Stock Exchange were in the public gallery, unable to believe their luck that the joke had gone this far and they were determined to give it a leg on whenever the pace seemed to slacken. Pat said afterwards that the man he felt sorry for was his opposite number, the plaintiff's counsel. 'How he managed to control his own emotions, and give any credence to the business, is something I'll never be able to understand.' When it came to his cross-examination he was short and to the point, 'Has not the name Blennerhasset been used for years by comic writers, both here and in America?'

'I have since found out it has been used in *The Bab Ballads*, and by Mark Twain.'

'Is the portrait in the advertisement in the least like you?'

This was a tricky one, as the public gallery was quick to realise. Mr Blennerhasset could not say 'yes', since most of the pictures depicted him as a maniac; if he said 'no' his case would sink further into the mire, so he asked if he need answer the question. There were derisive calls from the gallery at that.

'Do you play Yo-Yo?'

'No.'

'Have you ever played golf at Walton Heath?'

'No.'

'So you have never holed a putt?'

'No.'

'Have you ever eaten lobster at Pimms'?'

'Yes.'

'Apart from the name, is that the only matter in which you resemble the gentleman in the advertisement?' And the final question,

'Do you know of a living person who has thought a penny

the worse of you because of the advertisement for Yo-Yo?'

It was shortly after this, when Mr McNully was giving evidence, that the judge stopped the case. He held that the alleged libel was only an advertisement, and not capable of a defamatory meaning.

It was strange that those that came to mock, didn't stay to jeer. They were reduced to an almost sad silence by the collapse of their stout party. As Theo said afterwards, 'In the Stock Exchange at any rate, the joke has gone sour. I don't think he'll be troubled there any more.' But it was an expensive way to scotch a snake, for the costs were not small.

One day one of Theo's pupils came out of Theo's room chuckling. He told me that Theo was behaving like a spider, 'He's crawling all over the office floor.' 'What do you mean?' I asked. 'I suggest you go and see for yourself,' I made some excuse for doing so, and sure enough there Theo was on the floor on his hands and knees surrounded by various piles of papers and books, moving sometimes forward, sometimes crabwise, among them. He looked up, 'Oh, it's you, what do you want?' he asked, almost crossly. I delivered some unimportant message, then said, 'What on earth are you doing, sir?' 'Doing,' he replied, 'I am trying to sort out some semblance of order, in a case which unless a legal miracle happens, is liable to occupy us for months. It is the case of the Diamond Syndicate.' It was one I already knew a bit about, for I had been in frequent communication with the solicitors and had received large bundles of papers from them which Theo was now in the process of 'sorting out'.

The case of the United Diamond Fields of British Guiana against the Diamond Syndicate must be one of the most fascinating, seemingly difficult, yet in the event simply resolved, in the annals of law. It was settled by the fusion of a fine lawyer's mind, and the patience and courage of a great pleader. It didn't need the legal miracle that Theo had wished for. The plans were carefully laid before the case went to court. The events were complex, but I will try and put them as briefly and succinctly as I can.

The Diamond Syndicate originated in the days of Cecil Rhodes when men like the Barnatos and Joels formed it; realizing that the value of diamonds lay in their scarcity, they therefore decided to restrict their distribution. This meant that they had to control all diamond production. For years they were successful. In 1925 diamonds were discovered in British Guiana, and the large quantities on the market attracted the attention of the Syndicate. Eventually an agreement was reached between the United Diamond Fields of British Guiana Limited and the Diamond Syndicate whereby the company agreed to sell all its diamonds to them. Unfortunately for the company they also agreed that a Mr Oppenheimer, who represented the Syndicate, should be given the position of their technical adviser, and it was he, and only he, who could regulate the price paid to them for diamonds by the Syndicate. Nor was the company allowed to see the Syndicate's books, which meant that they could not check the prices they were given against the prices at which the diamonds were sold. So they were completely at the mercy of the Syndicate. They were shown none. Mr Oppenheimer continually reduced the price the Syndicate was prepared to pay until it became so low that the company could no longer trade at a profit, and it faced ruin.

On the British Guiana company's board was a man of notable ability, Victor Coen. Although he knew nothing about diamonds, he felt that the company was being cheated, and decided to bring the matter to the courts. Mr Oppenheimer did his utmost to persuade Coen to go to arbitration, but was refused. In May 1929 two actions were begun, one for conspiracy and fraud against the Syndicate and Mr Oppenheimer, and the other for an account against the Syndicate. The damages claimed were £200,000. The Syndicate's financial resources were limitless, so their strategy was to prepare for a lengthy and costly trial, to flood it with so much evidence that it would render a verdict extremely difficult, if not impossible to reach, for in the end the jury would be incapable of realising what it was they were supposed to try. Theo therefore decided from the start to find one incident on which to concentrate attention, and this was what he was doing on the floor when I had interrupted him.

There were some four thousand letters alone, apart from

hundreds of other documents, so it was like looking for a needle in a haystack. But Theo found it. The Syndicate had had to show some of their book entries to us, and among these was an entry for a sale of British Guiana diamonds at a certified profit of 17 per cent. Now Mr Oppenheimer had stated that the profit was only 5 per cent, and had used that fact to cut the price paid to the company by 10 per cent. There was no explanation for this discrepancy. Theo immediately got in touch with Patrick Hastings, who was leading for us, and it was decided to stand or fall on this issue alone.

It was a risk that only two barristers of their calibre and standing could afford to take, for if it didn't succeed our clients could have come down on us and accused us of giving too little attention to the mass of detail; as it was they must have been perturbed and anxious when they came into court and compared the piles of papers and books on their opponents' desks, with those on ours. The action came to trial on 17 March 1930 before Mr Justice McCardie and a special jury. Patrick Hastings explained the story in a few words, telling the jury that there was only one small point which would decide the case, and which would not take them more than a few minutes to understand; Mr Oppenheimer's certificate was either honest or not. He warned them that they would have to listen to days of cross-examination on matters that he considered irrelevant, but that eventually the defendants would have to explain Mr Oppenheimer's certificate.

When the Syndicate's advisers, led by Mr Stewart Bevan, heard this, they gave signs of being overjoyed as did Mr Norman Birkett, who was appearing for Mr Oppenheimer. Their joy was not well-founded.

We were fortunate in having as substantially the only evidence to support our case that of Mr Victor Coen, whom Partick Hastings later described as the best witness he'd ever seen in the box. He was cross-examined for four days by Mr Bevan, was never at a loss for a date, a fact or an answer; he never showed temper and was always courteous. It was interesting that during all that time no mention was made of Mr Oppenheimer's certificate. Then it was up to Mr Birkett, who also worked on

Mr Coen for four days, without any success. Finally, however, he had to come to the certificate. To my mind he had left it too long, for both judge and jury must by now have become impatient to hear of it, and suspicious that any mention of it had been delayed so long. I think I detected a sigh of relief from everyone in court, when Norman Birkett said, 'Now I want to refer to Mr Oppenheimer's certificate.' Birkett's attempt to explain it was that after the sale of the diamonds the purchaser had been dissatisfied with his bargain, and although the Syndicate could not repay the money, Mr Oppenheimer, out of the kindness of his heart, bought them back himself. This of course did nothing to determine the truth or falsity of the certificate, and the judge immediately spotted this. He interposed:

'Do you mean Mr Birkett that Mr Oppenheimer bought them back for himself, or for the Syndicate, or what?'

'He brought them back for himself. Even if it was done wrongfully and mistakenly, it cannot be a fraud.'

'If it was secret, of course, I say no more than it might well be the grossest fraud. Where are the accounts by which he adjusted this transaction?'

'With all due deference, no such accounting would be necessary.'

'Mr Birkett, are you going to suggest that the books, showing a sale, do not represent the truth of the matter, mark this, at the moment when the certificate was given?'

'Yes, my lord.'

'Is the truth contained in any other documents or document whatsoever?'

'It is, my lord.'

'But not entered in your books. Just reflect on what you are saying, Mr Birkett, not entered in your books! Is that what you mean? If you say that, it means that these accounts that you are putting before me, are not worth the paper they're written on. Reflect, Mr Birkett. At this stage the action may assume a grave aspect.'

Finally Mr Justice McCardie went on to say, 'Let me tell you at once, Mr Birkett, that curtains of ingenious suggestions, or veils of ingenious suggestions, will be no good in the end as far as I am concerned. I shall put them aside, and get at the truth and I am sure the jury will assist me in that.'

Those words of course were music to our ears. The case was over. In fact, it lingered on for a few days, the defence needed the time to put their house in order. The question on every lawyer's lips, and that included many outside the law courts, was 'when is Mr Oppenheimer going to appear, to give his side of the story?' He never did. The excuse given was that he was too unwell. The situation had now arisen that if he did appear, and the verdict was given against him, the papers concerning the case might well be sent to the public prosecutor, and he could have been faced with a prosecution for fraud, never to one's advantage, win or lose. Instead, the defendants threw in the towel. They said they were anxious to make good any loss the company had suffered, but could only agree to pay in the action for account, in that way scrubbing out any admission of fraud on the part of Mr Oppenheimer. To Mr Coen it was a matter of indifference, so long as the claim was paid. The defence, of course, tried to argue over the settlement, but Mr Coen proved as a good a bargainer as he was a witness, and they paid in full. What particularly interested me in a most fascinating case was that Mr Oppenheimer was able to get away scot free. It gave proof to that saying that the Law is like a spider's web, it catches the flies and the gnats, but the wasps and the hornets get through.

Although this next case was not one that concerned Theo, it illustrates another neat piece of strategy by Pat Hastings. It was used at the trial of Mrs Barney, a *cause célèbre* of 1932; a murder in the smart set. Mrs Barney was accused of shooting her lover Stephens. The defence was that she had threatened suicide and in the struggle to take the pistol from her, Stephens had been killed. One of the witnesses for the prosecution was Sir Bernard Spillsbury, the eminent pathologist, and such was his standing and reputation in the courts that many prosecutors treated him almost as God, and his effect on juries was thought by some to be more telling than the judge's summing-up. He was also allowed to sit in court during a trial, and prosecuting counsel would sometimes put the following question to him, 'Sir Bernard, you have heard the defence put forward on behalf of the prisoner. In your opinion is it consistent with the results of your examination?' To which the only reply could be, 'No.' So at the beginning of the trial Pat asked that Sir Bernard should not be allowed to remain in court at the opening of the case, and the calling of the evidence. The judge, Mr Justice Humphries, agreed. When Sir Bernard was called to give evidence it was purely on medical grounds. He had not heard the theory of suicide, and so no question could be put to him on that or any other theory. He was not cross-examined.

After the case was over, Sir Patrick Hastings took a holiday in France. When he returned he came round to our chambers, and was congratulated on his conduct of the case. 'The verdict was nearly the death of me,' he said. 'I was driving on the road from Boulogne to Paris, when a sports car, with a woman at the wheel, came round a corner very fast, and on the wrong side. It missed me by a whisker. I got a glimpse of the driver. It was Mrs Barney.'

Well over fifty per cent of Theo's cases were for newspapers, and concerned libel or slander. For seven years he dealt with the writs involving *John Bull*. Readers were invited to write in to the paper if they had a grievance. It was a sort of poor man's letter to *The Times*. The letters were printed often without checking facts. This resulted in over a hundred writs a year, which Theo had to deal with; yet while he was employed by *John Bull*, no case ever went to court. All cases were settled, and the fact that the paper continued with its policy for this length of time must reflect on Theo, since the amounts he was able to agree in settlement made it worth their while.

Although he made a good annual income from this work, others made more. There was a firm of speculative solicitors whose principal was Edmond O'Connor. His brother Martin was a barrister and, although his behaviour might not have been in the highest tradition of the Temple, he was a genial and likeable cove; as a comedian he would have done well on the halls. Edmond O'Connor would scan the paper, and if he thought that a person had been libelled, he would write to him saying so, and offer to take on his case speculatively, that is to say, with payment by results. There would be a rather larger payment if the firm succeeded than would normally be paid to a lawyer. In nine cases out of ten, therefore, Theo would be dealing with Martin O'Connor over the settlement. Often Theo would be prepared to settle without having received a brief, but Martin would have none of it. 'No brief, no settlement. If I don't get a brief I won't get any money out of it. That cunning brother of mine will see to that.' Theo would shake his head at him. 'You're a rogue, Martin,' but the two Irishmen would laugh together. The settlements were never too high. After all Martin didn't want to kill the goose that laid the golden egg.

However, the goose was eventually killed. John T. Monks, the solicitor who handled most of Odham's work, either died or retired, and his cases were given to another firm who decided to fight some of them. They lost and the damages and costs were so high that it was decided to change the nature of *John Bull;* it became more respectable and conformist, but it lost its circulation.

Theo had one golden rule for libel or slander. When the client came to see him, his first question would be, 'Is what has been said true?' and if the answer, however faltering, could be interpreted as yes, he would then say, 'Under those circumstances, I should go away and treat it with the contempt it deserves.'

I remember when Quintin Hogg was a pupil, he came in one morning convinced that a newspaper had libelled him. He went to Theo for advice. 'This is what you do, Quintin,' Theo said. 'Go round and demand to see the editor of the paper, and take another pupil with you. Insist on having an apology printed, and don't come back until you've got a promise from him.' He followed Theo's advice and got the necessary promise. Little did the editor know that he had been confronted by a future Lord Chancellor and a Chancellor of the Exchequer, for as his companion Quintin had chosen Peter Thorneycroft.

The law can also be used to stop slanderous gossip. At the time of the Simpson affair, after Mrs Simpson had obtained her divorce, it was rumoured that her ex-husband had received £40,000 to agree to be named as the guilty party. To prevent this rumour getting any credence, a young lady was found who assented to allow herself to be prosecuted for uttering this slander. She pleaded guilty and gave a full apology, saying that she now realised it was a pack of lies. It gave Mr Simpson the chance to go into the box, make a full denial of the story and to say that he accepted the lady's apology. The case received wide coverage in the newspapers, and the public's conscience was quieted.

There are cases, of course, where newspapers, having published something which they know to be true, make a public withdrawal rather than allow the case to go forward, because they realise that the money and the forces against them are so big and strong that it would not be worth their while fighting an action.

Theo was concerned with a case that must rate as one of the most notorious of the century. Hundreds of newspaper articles have been written about it, some quite recently; books followed and there has even been a musical play, 'The Stiffkey Scandals of 1932'. One day, early in 1932, Harold Davidson, a diminutive clergyman in his late fifties, walked into our chambers. He had a large nose and an even larger personality, which was reflected through his mesmeric blue eyes and his eager sparkling manner. If he was worried about the fact that he was shortly to face grave charges concerning his moral character, he didn't show it. In fact we were not concerned in the main case, which was held at a Consistory Court at Church House, Westminster, where he was charged with mixing with women of low character, under the guise of saving their souls. Ours was a preliminary skirmish concerning contempt of court. The rector had an appointment with Theo, and a conference with solicitors representing the *Daily Herald*, but had arrived half an hour early, so he spent the time chatting with me. I liked him instantly, despite what I had heard, and was fascinated by his easy-flowing conversation. When eventually he was called into Theo's room, I found myself comparing his predicament with that of the Gladstone brothers, and their case against Captain Wright, and wishing him the same success. The cases had a great similarity; the rector had cited Gladstone as his inspiration: 'Many years ago, Mr Gladstone visited a clergyman friend of my father's. I have always remembered what this friend said of Gladstone's attitude towards fallen women, and I made up my mind to help them as far as I could.'

Our part in the case was of small consequence. Because of its nature, Fleet Street journalists, smelling a naughty and scandalous story which would titillate their readers, burrowed around for as much background material as they could find. In their enthusiasm some went astray, possibly unaware that pre-trial comment applied as much to Church courts as it did to Criminal and Civil courts. One offender was the *Daily Herald*, which had published two articles. The first was an interview with an attractive West End actress, who was appearing in Noel Coward's musical 'Cavalcade' at the Drury Lane Theatre. She said that the rector had helped her many years before, and that she had only ever heard good of him. She added that she was quite happy when she was at the theatre to leave her fifteen-year-old daughter in his care. The second was a more serious complaint. Rose Ellis complained that she had been bribed by detectives into making an untrue statement against Davidson. In conference, it was decided by Theo and Norman Birkett to admit the contempt, to apologise but to plead ignorance of the rules against which the *Herald* had offended. When the case went to the High Court the fine imposed was £50, a price which the newspaper no doubt felt was more than reasonable for the privilege of having published the articles.

I followed the trial with keen interest. While a lot of mud was slung at poor Stiffkey – by now the man and the place had become as one in the public's mind – his defence was able to show the good work he'd done over many years. At one time it had been largely confined to boys' clubs in the East End and pastoral work in connection with the Dockland Settlement Scheme. Later he had become a chaplain of the Actor's Church Union, and there were few stage doormen to whom he was not a familiar figure. Later still he extended his work to helping women of the streets, which earned him the title 'The Prostitute's Padre'. It was perhaps ironic that the evidence which probably told most against him came about through his friend Rose Ellis. He had allowed himself to be photographed in a compromising position with her daughter. She was naked, except for a shawl, which was shown to be held together by the rector's fingers. It was produced dramatically by the prosecution, and he was asked to explain it. 'Yes, that was a mistake, it should have been pinned,' was the only answer he could give. He was found guilty, and later was deprived of his living before the altar of Norwich Cathedral. I've always thought that that ceremony must have been the nastiest for anyone in the Church of England to have had to perform. Forgiveness is, after all, the cornerstone of the Christian faith; publicly to deny it in God's house seemed a denial of that faith.

Poor old Stiffkey became an entertainer, so joining the profession that had helped to discredit him. He allowed himself to be exhibited in a barrel on Blackpool's Golden Mile, and drew large crowds. Finally, he took part in an exhibition with two caged lions. His death was that of many a Christian martyr. He was mauled by one of the lions, and two days later died. It was with great sadness that I read of his death. This was unprofessional of me. Those of us concerned with the Law should be like those concerned with medicine, dispassionate and divorced from personal involvement. It is the only way to survive.

I worked with Theobald Mathew for twenty-three years, some of them my most impressionable ones, so perhaps it is not surprising that for me he was the essence of the Law, and of a gentleman. I have served men of greater repute since, but they will, I know, excuse me my idol. It is a measure of the regard in which his work was held that at the age of seventy-two he was as busy, if not busier, than he'd ever been. I cannot, however, subscribe to the view that it was work that killed him; he thrived on it. Had he retired earlier or tried to restrict his output, I don't think he would have survived so long.

The first signs of any trouble same towards the end of 1938, when he complained about his eyes. 'My sight seems to be failing me, Sydney. I think I'll go and see an optician.' This he did, and got some new spectacles. They helped at first but his sight deteriorated again and his handwriting became almost indecipherable. He then saw his doctor, who suggested a long holiday.

It was now that Theo saw the writing on the wall. 'Sydney,' he said, 'I think I have the same complaint that my father died of, when he was my age.' He took the holiday, though he insisted on finishing one big case before he went. We were lucky in having in chambers another junior, Hubert Hull, who was experienced in the same kind of work, so when clients asked for Theo I was able to pass them over to him. During his absence I learnt the art of forgery. He had left without making any provision for the signing of cheques, so I copied his signature in order to pay the necessary bills. I'm glad to say there was never a query from the bank.

Theo returned to us for a time, but it soon became apparent that he would have to give up. When I went to see him I was astonished how he had deteriorated. He tried a few flashes of wit, but somehow our laughter had a hollow ring about it. When he asked me to tell him how things were going in chambers, he said, 'Be careful, Sydney. If you tell me that everything's running smoothly, it will make me think my presence there was un-necessary. If, on the other hand, you say everything is in chaos I shall jump of bed, and return immediately.' My next visit was two days before he died. His condition had worsened, he was nearly blind and found difficulty in talking. I spent about a quarter of an hour as it were reciting a monologue, just telling him any-thing and everything I could think of, since conversation was out of the question. It wasn't made any better by the interruption of his nurse, who spoke to him as if he were a baby. It made me angry. I wanted to shout at her, 'Don't you realise you're talking to a man who had one of the finest brains in the Temple.' I went back to Paper Buildings, and told Hubert Hull the bad news. He went to see him the following day, and was also able to speak to his doctor; on his return he reported that Theo was unlikely to live through the night. He did, but only just; he died on 20 June 1939.

A Requiem Mass was held at Brompton Oratory on the morn-of a working day in term time. The building was packed with members of all branches of the Law. The High Court postponed their sittings until eleven o'clock so that judges and counsel could attend. It was the greatest assembly of the cream of the legal profession I ever saw, though when it was over I heard someone remark drily, 'Theo would have been amused to see so many of his favourite bores in attendance.' One other memory I have; as Do and I left the Oratory Theodore Goddard, head of one of the biggest firms of solicitors, and a client of Theo's for many years came up to me. 'Sydney, I just want you to know that Mr Mathew's death will make no difference to our association. I think you will find that as much work as ever will be coming your way.' It was a very kind and generous remark for him to make, and he was as good as his word. I was glad that later as I shall recount I was able, in some small measure, to repay his kindness.

Some little time before his death, Theo decided to augment our chambers, and Richard O'Sullivan, KC, had been asked to join us. So since Hubert Hull had been doing Theo's work during his holiday and illness, little reorganization was required. Somehow Theo's personality lingered. I am not a fanciful man, but I was not as astonished as some when I arrived at our chambers one morning to hear the following story from Mrs Hayden, Florrie, our laundress, who was in hysterics. It appeared that she had arrived as usual to do the cleaning. 'After all these years, Mr Sydney, it becomes a matter of routine, your mind isn't really on what you're doing. So when I went into Mr Mathew's room, and saw him sitting in his chair, I thought nothing of it. I said I was sorry for intruding on him, and told him I'd come back later. He smiled at me, then got up, went over to the fireplace and sat down in his armchair. It wasn't until I came out that I realized what I had seen, it was Mr Mathew's ghost. Oh, Mr Sydney, what shall I do, I'll never be able to work here again.' Now although some people laugh when I tell them the story today, no one at Number 4 did at the time. Florrie also cleaned for Judge Leonard. He talked to her, and was able to comfort her, and afterwards told me that he was convinced that she was sincere in everything that she had said. It was also fortuitous that during that same morning we were visited by the nuns, who had come to convey their condolences on Theo's death. I think that they made Florrie feel proud that

Theo should have chosen to manifest himself to her. We always used to talk about it afterwards as 'Florrie's great day'. I have never been prepared to commit myself on the matter; all I know is that from then on there was no longer that strong feeling of Theo's presence in our chambers.

I must now retrace my steps, and return to the year 1928 when I took over from Wootton and became chief clerk. I was comparatively young for the position, but I'd been lucky. I had worked for Packer, the go-getter who had taught me well and worked me hard. Then in contrast I was under Wootton, who was content to pass as much work as he could on to me. I'd accepted it willingly, again because of Packer's advice, so the new job bore no terrors for me. I suppose what hit me most was that from the very humble wage packet of twenty-eight shillings a week, my earnings jumped to around £500 a year, and I knew that from any future work that came into our chambers I would soon be getting a percentage. It took me some time to adjust to my new-found wealth. First I decided to try and look the part. I bought a new suit – black coat and vest with striped trousers – a black bowler and wore a winged collar with a black bow tie. I also exchanged my soft shoe shuffle for a manly stride. It didn't pass unnoticed. I was teased by some of my friends at first, but like myself they soon got used to my new image.

When Macnaghten left Hubert Hull took over his room. Theo became sole head of chambers and was our tower of strength. Longland, O'Donnel and Ludlow shared the remaining room. We got our fair share of any work that was going, and although we boasted no great or famous names, our clients were sound, the work good and we had a part in many cases that caught the public's eye, as well as others that kept our reputation among solicitors. I think everyone was reasonably satisfied with the results I was able to show. They didn't say so of course. The only clue I got was from Wootton, who came in from time to time to collect his percentages, as the money came in for work that was accredited to him. He had access to the books, and would

96

regularly complain at the amount of money I was getting, 'You're making a hell of a lot more than I did when I was here, or than I'm getting now.' As a judge's clerk Wootton was on a fixed salary of £400 a year.

When it became obvious that Theo would not be returning to chambers, Richard O'Sullivan joined us. He was a leader of some considerable experience, and had been elected Recorder of Derby the previous year. He had also prosecuted in the IRA trial of 1939, when a bomb had been planted in Coventry killing two people and wounding two others. Four people were arrested, two were hanged and the others imprisoned.

It was shortly after he came into our chambers that I received a telephone call for him late one evening. In those days we didn't ask who was on the other end, so I put the call straight through to O'Sullivan's room. A moment or two later he came out looking white under the gills, and said, 'I'm off, Sydney. I've just had a call from some Irish scoundrel, saying that he's going to get me. I suggest you warn the others, and that everyone else leaves as well.' Austin Longland was the only one still in apart from my junior. When I told him he suggested I rang the city police and gave them the details. He didn't stay to find out the results, but quickly made off home. So did my junior. The police didn't take long in sending someone round, even though it was only a young constable. 'They've probably planted a bomb,' was his theory, so we searched the offices, looking for any unfamiliar object. We didn't find one. 'Let's look in the hall in between the chambers, there may be something there,' the constable then suggested. There wasn't. Suddenly he stiffened. 'Listen,' he cried. We both held our breaths. 'Can you hear it, something's ticking?' 'It's not a clock,' I replied. 'Then it must be a bomb. Go and ring the station, and tell them to get help here quickly.' I did this and returned to the corridor, but the constable was nowhere to be seen. I shouted for him; he was outside and had put some distance between himself and our building. If the bomb was going off he was determined to be a witness, not a casualty. We waited there together for some considerable time. At last a man arrived, who seemed to know what he was doing.

We took him into Number 4, and once agains held our breaths, while we listened to the ticking. Our expert began laughing. 'That's no bomb,' he said, as he traced a small pipe along the wall, 'it's a time switch to control the lights.' The constable and I, feeling a little more than sheepish, began breathing easily again. 'I suggest you cut off home now,' the expert said to me, 'we'll sort something out in the morning,' and he and the constable left me to lock up.

The police were up bright and early, for when I got to chambers there were two plain clothes men and a constable on the doorstep. It had been decided by higher authority that the constable would be on guard outside, and that the two men would be inside our chambers, one to keep watch on the rooms and the other to tail O'Sullivan whenever he went out. This was all right so long as Richard confined himself to the City, but as they were quick to point out, they had no jurisdiction outside its boundaries, so if the barrister went into the West End for his lunch, or whenever he went home, he would be an unguarded target. Another man was therefore sent from the Special Branch of the Metropolitan Police. The uniformed constable outside resented that the other three policemen were able to sit inside in comfort. Then the Special Branch Officer took out a revolver, 'Where did you get that?' the two city policemen enquired. 'It's an issue on jobs of this kind,' was the reply. When the others went back to the station, they raised a complaint. It didn't do them any good, but it caused a rift in the lute. After being followed around by a human bloodhound for a short time, O'Sullivan found it restricting and aggravating. 'I can't call my body my own,' he said half jokingly, to me, but I could see it was getting on his nerves. Once he arrived back at our chambers unaccompanied, 'I've managed to give him the slip, Sydney.' I couldn't be amused for by now there had been a number of bombs placed around the West End, and pillar boxes were regularly being blown up. It seemed that he might be in more danger now, and I said so. 'Yes, I expect you're right,' he agreed wryly, then he brightened, and said, 'But supposing I had a fancy woman, what on earth would I do then?' I must say the situation was irritating me, our tea bill had tripled, there always seemed to be a kettle on the boil and the constant chatter or bickering interfered with work. When one of them brought a book in I looked forward to some relief; it was the stories of Guy de Maupassant, the nearest we got to pornography at that time, but my work was frequently interrupted with 'Listen to this bit, Syd, it's real spicy.' When war was declared IRA activities ceased, and the police were removed. It was, I thought, ironic that it took a war to give me a bit of peace.

Not unnaturally thought and talk of war had affected our lives in the Temple. I think many of the younger barristers, particularly those who were finding work hard to come by, were almost looking forward to it. Although I was optimistic I prepared for the worst. I knew that my poor eyesight would preclude me from joining the services, so I enlisted for training as an ARP warden. Most nights when I returned home to Petts Wood I'd go for instruction in first aid, the recognition of poison gases and the like, so that I was fully qualified when war was declared. It took me by surprise. When I considered what the First World War had cost in lives and suffering, I couldn't believe that whatever the rights or wrongs were we would venture into such a holocaust again. Lawyer-like I was confident, even until the last minute, that it would be settled out of court.

Chapter Six

After the early excitement of an air raid warning hot upon Mr Chamberlain's declaration of war, everything seemed to settle down quite peacefully. We were not subjected to the expected bombardment, and the period of the phoney war gave us a sense of security. Domestically and in chambers though, there were sudden and sweeping changes. I arranged for Do and Carol-Anne to go to Harrogate in Yorkshire, which allowed me to concentrate on my 'mistress', the Temple.

Since every man was as wise as the next in determining what was likely to happen, I sat back, surveyed the scene and made my plans. Prospects didn't look too good. Hubert Hull stayed with me only a short time, and then went to the Prize Court, to be concerned with shipping, Richard Ludlow had joined the forces, and O'Donnel, who had once been a regular officer, was immediately called up and eventually promoted to the rank of Major General, so I was left with O'Sullivan and Longland. Longland, who was on the Oxford circuit, was making noises about leaving for the country, and O'Sullivan was spending much of his time on government work and ultimately went to the Isle of Man, where he was responsible for the examination of the alien detainees who were held there.

It seemed to me that all we could do was sit tight, pull in our belts and wait. I was lucky; over the hall from us were Colonel Carthew's chambers. He had been called up but one day he paid me a visit. 'I'm in a bit of a hole, Sydney,' he said, 'my chief clerk, Hellman, has enlisted and gooduns are not easy to come by at the

100

moment. I understand you're not too busy, and I'd be glad if you would take over the work of my chambers. I can only offer you half fees, as we've promised to pay Hellman the other half.' I accepted readily, partly because it was a time when it seemed only right to give help wherever it was needed, and partly because it would enable me to keep our own chambers going. Three juniors were left in Carthew's practice, one of whom, Anthony Pereira, was at that time something of an expert on Hire Purchase Law. Shortly after this I had another stroke of luck, which was to affect not only the war years but provide our chambers with stability and distinction for many years afterwards; Kenneth Diplock came to see me and asked if he could return to us. He had been one of Theo's outstanding pupils and had remained a friend of his, and partly as a result of this affinity felt a strong wish to come back. I welcomed him with open arms. Here I knew was a man I could work for. I had followed his progress since he had left us six years ago, and it was obvious that his brilliance, coupled with his infinite capacity for hard work, must evenutally lead him to one of the highest offices in the land.

To give a true picture of the man, I must describe his earlier life. He was the son of a Croydon solicitor, who specialised in Patent Law. He went to Whitgift School and then to University College, Oxford, where he studied chemistry, although it was always his purpose to go to the Bar. It was thought that his father's practice would provide Patent work for him there but his father died while he was still at Oxford so that put an end to that plan, and he was never to be concerned in a Patent case until he was sitting in the Court of Appeal. Kenneth and Quintin Hogg were contemporaries at Oxford, where for the first time their paths crossed, Quintin being President and Kenneth Secretary of the Union. But Diplock was the first of them to become a pupil of Mathew. I remember that when we met I was struck by his similarity to Fred Astaire; he had that same jaunty, almost cheeky look, and I later expected him to break into a tap routine whenever he came down the corridor. In a way I wasn't wide of the mark, that is if a dancer can be compared with a jockey, for he was a keen horseman; he hunted and was a frequent rider at the

Bar point-to-point races at their meetings at Kimble near Princes Risborough before the war, and after the war at Friars Wash in Hertfordshire. He never told me when he was likely to win so that I could have a bet and make a bit of money, which may or may not be an indication of his character. He was also a weight-watcher; he's as slim now as he was then and I put it down to his love and consideration for the horses.

It was apparent during his pupillage that he was bound for stardom; Theo extolled his work and never denied Kenneth the credit if ever he used his Opinions or Pleadings in cases. I remember that on one occasion during a conference with a client I was asked to go and find him. It was a big case and when the solicitor was told of Kenneth's part in it, he insisted that he be briefed as second junior to Theo; that is what makes news in the Temple, and the news spreads to clients. It was not surprising, therefore, that when his year with Theo was up, he stayed with us for a while devilling, and then, on the recommendation of Theo and myself, was able to join Valentine Holmes' busy and distinguished chambers. From there, after a year, he went on the Oxford Circuit as Marshall to the Honourable Mr Justice Travers Humphreys for two months, during which time he was able, as a personal assistant to the judge, to talk and learn a lot about Criminal Law. He later went to Leslie Scott's chambers, who subsequently became a Lord Justice, mainly working in the Court of Appeals and when after two years Percy Glover, a Silk from the North, took over from Scott he worked with him, particularly on cases concerning coal mining.

In 1939 Glover died suddenly and Hartley Shawcross became head of chambers, but for only a brief period until the war. It was then that Kenneth came to Number 4, eventually taking over as head of chambers, both of Carthew's and our own sets.

I learned and practised early in my life with the Bar the military maxim, 'always reinforce success, never attempt to reinforce failure', and so I gave Kenneth Diplock my absolute attention. He not only responded, he led the way. I was no clairvoyant; I already had an early indication of his potential work in terms of hard cash. During his first year as a barrister he'd earned £150; during his second this rose to £1000. It means little in money terms today, but it spoke volumes to me then. People will say, without meaning it unkindly, that it paid me to give my attention to those who brought in the money since I was on a percentage of their earnings. This is true, and when I say that when Kenneth Diplock accepted preferment to the Bench it meant a drop in my income of over £2500 a year, it gives them greater credence. But that was not what really mattered, either to myself or the barristers that I served; it was the love of the chase, the getting of good work, the fascination and the satisfaction of a job well done, win or lose. I am sure that Kenneth Diplock, and indeed all those others that I worked for would agree with this; in fact I got Kenneth's opinion second-hand, when a friend of mine reported that he had said, 'Sydney was singularly ungreedy, he refused to take from me more than what he regarded as the standard clerk's fees, which were probably out of date by the end of my career at the Bar.'

With the arrival of Diplock and our joining forces with Carthew, it looked as though we were now secure. Kenneth made worrying noises about joining up, but to my relief the army turned him down on medical grounds. It wasn't a lack of patriotism on my part, but it seemed to me that he was doing a much better job where he was than on a drill square.

After Dunkirk I think we all knew it wouldn't be long before the bombing began; somehow I never imagined that Hitler could possibly launch an invasion. Then the Battle of Britain brought the threat of air raids even nearer. I decided to sleep in the Temple during the week as it wasn't much fun going to an empty house in Petts Wood each evening. I bought a camp bed and slept in one of the rooms. I was also able to transfer as a Warden to the City, and to carry out my duties near the Temple.

When at last the bombs began to fall I was busy day and night. For my warden's work I came under the command of a Mr Lewis, a solicitor of the firm of Cripps, Harris & Co., and since Kenneth felt aggrieved at not playing a more active part in the war effort, he joined forces with us unofficially. Often when things got a bit hot, Lewis would sleep in an armchair in Number 4, and

I would make up a camp bed there for Diplock.

As the raids progressed it seemed that the Temple led a charmed life since we suffered little damage. On 9 September 1940, a bomb hit the clock tower of the library and damaged the structure of the building but it was a slight casualty when compared with the devastation in other places in the City.

Then on the night of Saturday, 10 May 1941, we were literally deluged with fire bombs as well as a few high explosives. It is hard now to separate it from the following night when we were again hit. When out of the shambles we were able to take stock of the destruction, we found that it included the Inner Temple Hall, the library, all the Benchers' rooms, Harcourt Building and the Temple Church, as well as of course many sets of chambers, which were either wholly or partially demolished. Stephen Benson, one of the barrister fire fighters, gives this picture, which also illustrates the courage and devotion of Roy Robinson, the Inner Temple Sub-treasurer, and his wife.

I found the church was well alight, the organ blazing and that part of the roof had fallen in. I went through the small door at the altar end. The safe there was locked so I couldn't save its contents. I brought out a Benchers' prayer book and an altar chair, to serve as mementoes of the old furnishings. With Roy Robinson and his wife, I then tried to save the Inner Temple library, and he and I worked a stirrup pump, with Mrs Robinson bringing water, until we had to give up. It was too hot and smoky, and the roof showed signs of collapsing.

Shortly after this Robinson was injured. We took him to a dressing-station from where later he bravely, but unwisely, returned and continued to help. While he was away Mrs Robinson and I succeeded in putting out a number of fires in King's Bench Walk with chemical extinguishers the water supply by now had failed.

By this time a bomb had exploded near to my own chambers at Number 4 Temple Gardens, and the whole row was ablaze. I debated whether to try and get my more valuable possessions out, but decided that I would not be able to face my fellow barristers if I put my own goods before theirs, so I left them to take their chance. I'm glad to say my virtue was rewarded, for the lower part of the building which included my own chambers, was saved! I used the time that I might have spent with my own property in saving some of the Inn's papers from the Treasurer's office and pictures from the Benchers' rooms.

Both Kenneth Diplock and I can vouch for the truth of Stephen Benson's story, and in particular of the part played by the Robinsons. It was as a result of those two nights that Mrs Robinson was christened the Florence Nightingale of the Temple.

We too were busy at the Inner Temple Hall, though we were late on the scene having occupied ourselves with the sets of chambers near to Number 4, which had caught fire. It was wasted effort for we only had stirrup pumps; many of the water mains and hydrants had been pierced or blown up by bombs, and those sources that were left were so stretched that only a trickle of water came from the hoses. Providentially, Paper Buildings was saved from all but superficial damage; though superficial damage in a raid of that nature meant that almost all our windows had been sucked out, doors wrenched from their hinges and books and papers littered everywhere. We were lucky in having flat roofs from which fire bombs could be easily discovered and shovelled onto the road below, to be quickly extinguished. The other miracle was that there was not one fatal casualty on either night.

When Monday morning dawned we were able to see the full extent of the damage. It was a frightening sight, made worse by the stench of burning and the smoke and dust that swept everywhere. Yet it was humbling as we looked at the charred documents and papers that had seemed so important two days before and now meant little or nothing to us. Sceptre and Crown had tumbled down, as King's Counsel and junior clerks rummaged among the rubble.

When the news got about that we had come through comparatively unscathed, I was bombarded with people who now wanted to take refuge in our chambers. The first on my doorstep was D. N. Pritt, KC, the Socialist MP for North Hammersmith; he was a brilliant lawyer, and a supporter of lonely, if not lost, causes. He brought his own clerk, so I didn't have many dealings with him. I grew to admire his mind, and the way in which he stuck to his principles when he might have had a more lucrative practice had he played along and looked after his own interests. Twenty-four hours after I had accepted Pritt, Gilbert Beyfus, another brilliant KC known familiarly as 'the fox', knocked at the door. I would have liked to have given him shelter too, but alas there was no room.

I was particularly glad to help Theodore Goddard, who had been so true to the word that he had given me at Theo's funeral, and had continued to pass work our way. His offices in Sergeants Inn had been hit and his staff were busy sorting through the wreckage. No one seemed to know what was going to happen, so I found the managing clerk and told him that I could accommodate a token staff while they were looking for new quarters. Theodore Goddard saw me that same afternoon. It was arranged that all messages would come through our office. I persuaded our barristers to work at home during the hours of 10 a.m. to 4 p.m., if they were not in court. Everyone co-operated, Goddards were able to keep on their feet, and in a few weeks moved to new premises. Money was of course offered, but not accepted. I think I took a few pounds for postage, but to have taken anything else at such a time would have been churlish. Who knew, we might have been looking for help any day.

It was strange that although all my time was spent in the City, which was the centre of the blitz, and for much of it I was outside on duty during the raids, the nearest I came to a bomb with my name on it was at my home in Petts Wood. I'd gone there one Sunday to give the place an airing, when I heard what was the unmistakable sound of a German bomber approaching. Then a string of bombs fell with their explosions coming closer. When it seemed certain that the next would fall on the house, there was a swoosh, the place rocked and then another bomb exploded on the other side of the railway line, which ran along the bottom of our garden. None of our windows caved in, neither was the house damaged in any way. I went outside to see if I could help the less

106

fortunate. Suddenly the back garden was ablaze, and a fountain of flames came from the middle of our lawn. What had happened was that the swoosh I had heard and the shaking of the house had been caused by an unexploded bomb which had hit the gas main and sparked off that pillar of fire. It took the brigade some time to get things under control, and it was many days before the disposal unit defused and removed the bomb which, had it exploded, would undoubtedly have blown me and the house to kingdom come. I was glad to get back that night to the comparative safety of the Temple.

I am not sure whether it was before or after the raids began that I was asked to take over yet another set of chambers in Number 3 Paper Buildings. I was approached by Bush James, KC, a leading Silk who specialised in divorce, as indeed did the others in his chambers. He also had lost his chief clerk, and I think was persuaded to see me by Ifor Lloyd, later Judge Lloyd, an ex-pupil of Theo's with whom he had always remained on good terms. Although I had no experience of divorce work, and made this plain, Bush James persisted and, I suppose partly through vanity, I agreed to take over. It was something I never regretted. It showed me a more human side of the Law, and introduced me to a wider set of clients. Another of Bush James' juniors was Victor Williams, a big man in every way, his heart was as large as his stomach and I believe I was able to help enhance his reputation.

For better or for worse the outbreak of war saw an upsurge in divorce cases, particularly among the upper crust. Previously a man's public and private life had been as one, and although it may not have been written into the terms of employment, many appointments were conditional on a spotless private reputation. The BBC under Reith was a typical example; even the innocent party in a divorce action had to resign from, or be sacked by, the Corporation. The same applied to the Guards and the Cavalry, and many other regiments of the line. Officers who had had to resign their commissions for this reason were now called to rejoin the colours. This created an anomaly, so the rules were now relaxed in the services and other professions and organisations were quick to follow suit.

107

I don't know whether the rule that women's names should not be mentioned in the mess applied to officers' clubs, but I was given to understand that for the first few months of the war the conversations at the Guards and Cavalry clubs mostly concerned pending petitions. Many of these cases were grist to the mill of Bush James' chambers, and the work came rolling in together with of course a number of defended cases. War conditions were not conducive to fidelity, families were split up and the arrival of military contingents of Commonwealth, French, Polish and others gave sex a different flavour for those with international tastes; later, of course, the Americans provided a banquet.

I was able to sense at once that potentially we had the best divorce chambers in the Temple, but I felt we were squandering our energies on too many small cases, on the Mr Browns and the Mrs Smiths, when we should be having Lord Brown and Lady Smith. I believed it was my duty to increase the reputation of those I served, so I spread it around solicitors that if they had an important client, I was prepared to put them at the top of the waiting list. I know it was bending the eithics a bit, but it was a matter between me and my own conscience; the barristers didn't know, though they must have occasionally wondered at the changing quality of their work. My ploy succeeded, cases poured in, and in particular it affected Victor Williams. He seized his opportunities, and with his flair and charm rose to the top. It also helped some of the younger barristers in my other chambers, as I had to hand a deal of the work to them. Later on Bush James became a High Court Commissioner, judging defended divorce petitions, and Ifor Lloyd, a County Court Judge. I'm not ashamed to say that within a comparatively short time we had skimmed the cream of the society work. Some of my enthusiasm must have brushed off on one of my juniors, for whenever he answered a telephone call from a client, his first question was, 'Ow much?'

Many judges took time to come to terms with the new attitude towards the Divorce Law. It had become accepted among lawyers that there was collusion in many cases, and that the Law was being used as a convenience. Some more enlightened and practical judges realised this, and played along with it, but others still continued rigidly to stick to the conventions, so the lists assumed great importance and there were either cheers or groans from the clerks, when they examined them. The King's Proctor remained a feared figure for if he found, or had evidence of, inchastity between the granting of a decree *nisi*, and a degree absolute, the divorce could become null and void. We had occasion to warn one of our clients, who was cohabiting with the lady who was to become his wife after his marriage had been dissolved, that he would have to cease living with her during this period. 'Good heavens, what on earth am I going to do?' 'I suggest you buy a goat,' said our barrister dryly. 'If that's your advice then, I will,' replied the client. The day the decree nisi came in I was instructed to send the following telegram: 'You can now kill the goat.'

I was fortunate to have two excellent junior clerks, Peter Ellis and Stanley Rogers. I also had a young man called Catt, a likable enough chap, but with an over-developed sense of fun. He took nothing seriously. He had a collection of 'joke props', imitation mice and spiders, that frightened the daylights of of Mrs Hayden, our laundress; tin blots of ink, which found their way into every room, and a variety of things which made rude noises when sat upon. He wouldn't have lasted in chambers in ordinary times, but I tolerated him because of the shortage of manpower. His cheekiness made him an unpopular figure at the Royal Courts of Justice, and particularly in the barristers' robing room. One morning he came back from the Courts with a swollen eye. When I questioned him it appeared that he had exasperated one of the counsel to such an extent that he'd taken a swipe at him. Today I suppose someone in Catt's position would bring an action for assault. He, however, took it philosophically; he felt he could afford to since he was a law unto himself. 'Don't you worry, Mr Sydney,' he said, 'I'll get even with him, and with the others who took against me.' He did. During one lunch break he went into the robing room and mixed up all the barristers' wigs and gowns. When they returned, with only enough time to get dressed and into court, they were in absolute confusion. It must have been a glorious sight. All the cases were delayed and there were red faces aplenty as counsels were berated by judges and unable to give acceptable reasons for their lateness.

I like to think that the next calamity which befell the robing room, although directly attributable to Catt, was accidental. Meat rationing was stringent during the war, offal was hard to come by and was mostly used for human consumption, so it was difficult to get meat for animals. One of the barristers had an arrangement with a nearby butcher, who from time to time would get him something for his dog. Catt had to collect the meat for this barrister. One morning Catt went for his parcel of meat, and then went straight to the robing room. The parcel was poorly wrapped, there was a shortage of paper as well at that time, so finding he had blood on his hands he put the package under the lockers while he washed. He collected some books and papers from one of our counsel and returned to chambers with them, but without the meat. It remained forgotten under the lockers. It rotted and began to smell. Counsel began to eye each other suspiciously. The smell became an unbearable stench, the authorities were informed, the room was closed and the plumbers moved in and set to work on the lavatories. Their efforts were fruitless. Carpenters arrived to unearth what was assumed to be a dead rat under the floorboards. As they were shifting the furniture into the corridor they discovered the offending parcel. By now it was in such a condition that no one could be sure what it was, and there were no volunteers to try and find out, so no blame fell on Catt. It was many months later, just before he joined the army, that he told me the tale. 'It was a mistake, Mr Sydney, honest it was. I just forgot about it,' he declared, but there was something in the way he said it, and the look on his face at the time, that left me unconvinced. Another nasty habit he had was his method for moving books from the courts. He would carry them to the corridor, and then imitating the Scottish game of curling, would sling them along the floor, showing not only a lack of respect for the Law, but also of lawyers, for one evening I had an irate counsel in my room, displaying a very swollen ankle. Apparently it had interrupted Catt's game and its owner had not only taken the knock, but also a tumble. Man shortage or no,

Catt would have had to go. I was able once again to be lenient; he had received his calling-up papers, and was leaving in a month's time. I felt that by passing him over to the tender mercies of a sergeant major, I would be doing both him and myself a favour.

It was when I took over Bush James' chambers that I first employed a woman on my staff. Heather Latimer was nineteen, and was not only stunning to look at but an excellent worker; it was her looks, though, that first attracted me. I felt that if we had to have a member of the opposite sex, her first qualification should be to adorn the Temple. I knew it would also give the clients a favourable impression. I'd first seen Heather while she was working for a Mr Valetta, another divorce counsel, and had chatted with her so that when she told me she was thinking of making a change, I had first refusal. She enjoyed working although she did tend to linger over lunch, which wasn't surprising, as almost every day some young officer would call for her and I became familiar with the badges of every regiment of the line, for she was fancy free and she told me she intended to stay that way throughout the war. She was the only secretary I have known who wore gloves when she typed; it was to protect her very elegant hands. Eventually she was taken captive by an American doctor and was married in the States. She remained a career woman, went into show business and presented a series of programmes on television.

After the raids on the Temple, as it was evident that the Law was in total disarray, it was decided to close the courts for six weeks, after which time our wounds still showed, but we were able to go into action again as a fighting force. I don't know whether it was because of his anger and bitterness caused by the raids, but Kenneth Diplock was now determined that, come what may, he was going to get into uniform. This time he applied to the RAF, but was again rejected on health grounds. There was no court of appeal, but this didn't stop such an astute lawyer. He went to his private doctor and was given some sort of medical certificate, which eventually enabled him to get into the Air Force, but for

111

home service duties only. I wasn't pleased, and I told him so. 'You'll end up like James Leonard, wasting your talents in the Judge Advocate General's Department, prosecuting the vicious and licentious airmen, when you could be doing some useful work for your country here.' 'You never know, Sydney,' he said, 'I may end up back in London' He received an immediate commission, went away for six weeks preliminary training and was indeed back in London at the end of that time. He had been appointed personal assistant to Air Vice Marshall William (Dickie) Dickson, who was then Director of Plans at the Air Ministry in Whitehall. After Dickson was replaced by John Slessor, later Air Chief Marshall, Kenneth stayed on his staff, working on Air Intelligence; finally he joined Lord Swinton, who was in charge of Security Executive. There, as he puts it, 'I helped to run a rather silly little secret racket until the end of the war.'

The great advantage from my point of view at that time was that he was back in the Temple, and not only back but anxious to put every moment of his spare time into his profession. By golly, did that man work! He was an inspiration to everyone, but he was also a worry. He would come back during his lunch break and immediately start on Opinions, either dictating or hammering away on a typewriter himself. He didn't bother about eating so long as there was always a cigarette to dangle from his lips. It was the same in the evening. He now had a young lady secretary, who was devoted to him as a spaniel to its master. There was something about Kenneth at that time that brought out the mother instinct in everyone near him, and that included me. His secretary was worried about his not eating and was often nearly in tears over it. 'He's got no ration cards. He sends them home to Buntingford. He's told Mrs Diplock that the RAF feed him, but they don't. What are we going to do?' She not only spoke to me, she went to Mrs Hayden, who in her gruff Cockney way cared for Kenneth as much as she did. So it ended up with all us putting something into the kitty. I don't think he ever knew what went on, but he was always grateful for anything that was done for him. I considered myself his batman, and told him so many years later. 'No, Sydney,' he said, 'I didn't think of you like that. When I was a pupil I looked on you as a jockey does his trainer. When I was in chambers I had a different image, you were a cross between the head porter and the head tutor of my Oxford college.'

By its nature Diplock's work was not of general interest. He was concerned with what is called lawyer's law, with Constitutional Law, Commercial Law, Boundary Commissions, Coal Mining. As he said there are two kinds of lawyers – those who are interested in ideas and those who are interested in people. He was interested in ideas, though he qualified this by saying, 'That doesn't mean that outside the law I am not interested in people.'

There were two cases in which he led in Pakistan just before he was appointed to the Bench in 1956. They were Constitutional cases, which were intensely fascinating to him and to other specialist lawyers; the entire procedures were published in a book by the academic barrister Sir Ivor Jennings, who was his junior at the time.

One case of Kenneth's stands out in my memory as having great human interest. It concerned the King (Kabaka) and parliament (Lukiko) of Buganda and took place in 1953. In order to understand it, it is necessary to know something of the history of Buganda. When, in the nineteenth century, British explorers were active in East Africa, Uganda was considered the key territory, of which Buganda formed a quarter of its area. Burton and Speke discovered that the source of the Nile was a huge lake in Uganda, and they named it Victoria. The source of the Nile was considered very seriously, for it was imagined that the Germans or French might get control of it, and in some way, though nobody explained how, alter the course of the river. It was therefore decided that the country should be absorbed into the Empire. The government forced treaties on the hereditary monarch, the Kabaka, and the lesser Ugandan chiefs by which they accepted British 'protection'. British policy was to develop it as an entirely African state, so there were few white settlers.

Shortly after the Second World War, with the rise of African nationalism, a progressive, reform-minded governor, Sir Andrew

Cohen, was appointed. He was incidentally one of the few Jewish members of the Colonial service. It was ironic that a man who supported African nationalism, self-government and unity, should bring about a situation where the traditionalist Africans (the Bugandans) and the modern nationalist Ugandans, were united into joint opposition against the British. This came about through the leading African personality in the country, the Kabaka of Buganda. Since their affiliation with Great Britain the Bugandans had formed their own parliament and administration, the Lukiko, and had become proud of their link with Britain. The country disliked change and resented their transfer from a protectorate under the Foreign Office to the administration by the Colonial Office, and what they considered their subordination to the Governor of Uganda. To Cohen Royal Buganda was an obstacle to converting Uganda to what he considered a proper nation state.

The Kabaka didn't help matters. He was what governments and administrations dislike more and more – a character. Known in newspaper headlines as 'King Freddie', he was part playboy and part serious politician. He had succeeded to the throne in 1939, at the age of fifteen, because he was the only son of a monogamous father to have been born in Christian wedlock. He went to Cambridge University, and to his intense pride was made an honorary captain in the Grenadier Guards. In the early 1950s, between excursions to Europe, he asked for the separation of Buganda from Uganda, and for its eventual independence under his sovereignty. His wishes went unheeded. In 1953 Oliver Lyttleton, then Colonial Secretary, implied in a speech in London that it was the Government's intention to set up an East African federation, including Uganda, complete with Buganda. An infuriated 'King Freddie', with the support of his Lukiko, and the backing of his subjects, began a campaign of non-co-operation. Cohen likewise lost his temper and, supported by the British government, arrested Freddie and put him on a plane to England. On his arrival he was told that he had to stay until further notice, but to make his exile tolerable he would be given £8000 a year tax free. Nobody, except those in Whitehall, was pleased. To

114

make matters worse Freddie's sister, Princess Nalanya, dropped dead from shock when she heard the news.

Cohen bade the Lukiko choose a new Kabaka; they refused to do so, nor would they, or the kingdom of Buganda, be coerced. Moreover the nationalist Africans in the rest of Uganda, who normally disliked Bugandan traditions and their policy of separatism, rallied to 'King Freddie's' cause, and the Colony was united against the common enemy, Britain. The billboards and banners in Uganda must have presented a comic sight, with pictures of 'King Freddie' resplendent in his Guards tie – the black St George in combat with the British dragon.

It was to this man and some of his ministers that I opened the door. They'd come to see Kenneth Diplock to find if they had any remedy for our government's behaviour in the courts. He discovered a way, and an action was brought in the High Court in Uganda, which claimed that the government had acted unlawfully. We failed in our action, but only on a technicality. We won a moral victory. An appeal was made to the Privy Council, and there was little doubt that we would have won. The case, however, had shown the British Government as having behaved badly, so it was decided to allow the Kabaka back, though to save face, the government asked in return for some changes in the constitution of Uganda.

Not unnaturally 'King Freddie' was cock-a-hoop. He didn't forget how much he owed to Kenneth Diplock, and his gratitude, and that of his ministers, was overwhelming. One morning, shortly, after the case had been concluded, Kenneth woke up to read in *The Times* that he had been appointed Constitutional Adviser to the Lukiko in their negotiations with the government about the new treaty. It was the first he had heard of this appointment. However, he agreed to it on the condition that he received no payment or fee. He told them that his reason for this was that if he thought they were acting foolishly, he could tell them so and refuse to proceed on their behalf. They thought this a splendid idea, not just because of the money. So it was that for the next three months when Kenneth came out of court, where he had been earning his living, as often as not there would be Bugandans waiting at chambers to have consultations with him about the next stage in negotiations with the Colonial Office, which Kenneth's friendship with the Colonial Secretary, Lennox Boyd, while not affecting the ultimate issue, undoubtedly made easier.

When eventually 'King Freddie' returned to Uganda Kenneth was invited to go with him and share in his triumph. He was given the red carpet treatment. I particularly mention it because this kind of action and this kind of tribute is rare in my experience of the Bar from our own countrymen; for it to be given so generously and openly by an African state was as much an indication of their code of behaviour as it was of Diplock's ability. History records that the Bugandan affair 'demonstrated conclusively that there existed such a thing as African public opinion, and that the British could be made to bend before it'. As I think my story shows this is not true. It took a High Court action to make the government bend. I cannot help wondering, therefore, how many 'munificent gestures by a far seeing democratic government' had their true origins at a similar source. As things turned out later, 'King Freddie' was again exiled, this time by an African National government, and Bugandan separatism was eventually defeated, with the disastrous consequences of which we are only too aware today.

A famous, if not notorious, client of Kenneth Diplock's was Calouste Gulbenkian, and he advised him, led by Cyril, later Lord Radcliffe, on a number of his oil deals. The fees were very good. Generally Kenneth went to Lisbon to see him at the Caleish Hotel. Only once do I remember Gulbenkian coming to Number 4. The meeting on that occasion wasn't too successful; he carried a lot of weight, and the chair he was given to sit on collapsed under him and he took a nasty tumble. In matters of law Gulbenkian believed in shopping around. He tried many of the leading members of the Bar, and divided them into three classes; those who had let him down, betraying him by acting for the other side, those who gave him unpalatable advice, and those who could do no wrong. Eventually Kenneth came into the second class, and as a result he was dropped; the only one to survive in the last class was Cyril Radcliffe.

116

To return to the war years; they were halcyon days for me. I was given the opportunity by running three sets of chambers to exploit the experience I had gained from a comparatively early promotion to chief clerk. I had widened my sphere of influence. I had a knowledge of almost every aspect of the law, and as a result had as clients many of the leading firms of solicitors of the time. My own confidence had been built up because I knew that others had confidence in me. I had the respect of those I served. Often solicitors would ring me and say, 'I don't suppose anyone in your chambers would be interested in taking this brief, but if they aren't can you recommend anyone else?' When that happens to a clerk he knows he's made it. It was a situation which might have done me harm. I think I was saved from it by my other love, the theatre. I had watched too many stars wax and wane not to realise that there is only one thing that is certain with any success in life, that is that it's going to end, and it's up to the individual, once having achieved it, to ensure that he retains it as long as possible. This in my experience can only be done by keeping a modest and clear head, anticipating change and being ready to meet it when it comes. It's easy to say, often difficult to do. I was very nearly a casualty. But I'm getting ahead of myself again.

A man of the theatre who was such a victim was the central figure of probably the *cause célèbre* of the Second World War, Ivor Novello. It was not a case in which any of my chambers had a direct interest, but it did for a time concern Sir Patrick Hastings; and his clerk, Matthew Robinson, knowing of my interest in the theatre was able to tell me part of the story; the rest was widely reported in the press.

The case illustrates the wisdom of that saying, 'Don't keep a dog and bark yourself'. Ivor Novello had been the romantic hero of British musicals since the First World War. He wrote his own scripts and music, and he probably had the greatest theatrical following of middle class playgoers of any man of his time. Shows like 'Perchance to Dream', 'Glamorous Night', 'Careless Rapture', 'The Dancing Years' are still performed to packed houses by amateur operatic groups over the country. Undoubtedly his most popular song, which he composed when he was a very

117

young man, was 'Keep the Home Fires Burning', a patriotic and nostalgic number which was sung throughout two world wars. It was therefore a deep and wounding blow, both to himself and his many friends and followers, when he was brought to court for what was an unpatriotic offence.

Petrol rationing was in force during the war, and though a limited number of coupons could be bought on the black market, it was fairly rigidly enforced both by law and individual conscience. Newspapers played watchdog to some extent, and as our losses of merchant vessels, particularly of oil tankers, grew larger, they asked for stricter stringency. The *Daily Mirror*, through its cartoonist Vicky, was perhaps the most demanding for swifter action, and greater penalties for those who offended. In 1942, when Ivor was appearing in 'The Dancing Years' at the Adelphi Theatre, he applied for extra petrol so that he could travel at weekends to his home Red Roofs, near Maidenhead. His application was refused. He spoke with some indignation about this, and his disappointment came to the ears of a woman fan. She claimed that she worked for a company doing important war work, and which was entitled to a large ration of petrol. She suggested to Ivor that if he transferred his car to her, she could put it on the list of the company, and he would obtain the petrol he required. This arrangement worked well until 8 October 1942, when Ivor had a telephone call from the managing director of the company, which technically held his car on its lists, wanting to know how it came to be there, and asking exactly what had been going on. Finding Ivor's explanations unsatisfactory he informed the petrol board, and police enquiries followed. Ivor and the woman were both charged with conspiring to commit offences against the Motor Vehicles Regulations. It was now that Pat Hastings came on the scene. As a friend and fellow playwright he was the obvious man to defend him. Pat advised Ivor to plead guilty, and to leave it to him to plead mitigating circumstances; that it had been a foolish mistake, made by a tired and busy man who had no knowledge of the gravity of his actions. This way, Pat argued, he would avoid the publicity of a full scale trial, would probably get off with a wigging and a heavy fine from the magistrate, and the case would quickly be disposed of. Pat did not get the brief, and the only possible explanation can be that his advice was unpalatable to Ivor.

There have been many speculations on exactly what influenced Novello. In the event he was defended by G. D. ('Khaki') Roberts, KC. Some unkind wit suggested that it was his fee for the brief of 100 guineas, as opposed to Pat's 250 guineas, which was the deciding factor. This of course was nonsense, for as far as Ivor was concerned money could have been of little consequence in the circumstances; in any case he was well known for his generosity. Others blamed his friends, who, unable to credit that he could do such a thing, persuaded him into believing in his innocence. He may, without their persuasion, have thought that he was a victim of some plot to discredit him, and that by pleading guilty he would smear the public image that he held so dear, and so wanted the opportunity to go into court to clear himself. Whatever or whoever it was that led him to his decision to defend was wrong, and the results were disastrous.

The courtroom at Bow Street was as packed on the morning of the 13 April 1943 as the theatres he had appeared in throughout the war. If those assembled in the court expected the nobility of performance they were accustomed to getting from Ivor, they were to be very disappointed. From the moment he stepped into the box, the case was lost. He made the most appalling witness, hesitant and mumbling, even when answering 'Khaki' Roberts; and floundering and evasive to Laurence Austin Byrne, who was prosecuting. The tactics couldn't have been worse. He appeared to want to shift the blame onto the woman and it seemed as if he was prepared to sacrifice a friend to save his own skin. He was sentenced to two months imprisonment while she was fined £50. This in itself showed that Pat Hastings had been right in his advice, for she must have been considered the principal conspirator.

Ivor was not immediately committed to jail; an appeal was lodged. It was heard at the London Sessions, Newington Butts. It was only partially successful; his sentence was halved and he was led away to serve it at Wormwood Scrubs. Gossip about the

119

case was as rife in the Temple as elsewhere. Laurence Byrne, who had prosecuted, was convinced that Ivor had sentenced himself by palpably lying when under oath, and by trying to cast the blame. Others insisted that 'Khaki' Roberts had been the wrong kind of counsel for such a case, with his heavy, ponderous style; and agreed, although they had no knowledge of it, with Pat Hastings' opinion. 'Khaki' defended himself by saying that Harold McKenna, who had been the presiding magistrate, was a tough nut, not given to leniency, and that Novello would never have got away with it. Ivor's friends were loyal to him, but he always felt he had let them down. Some say that he never recovered from his imprisonment and the disgrace that went with it and that it caused his early death. No one concerned with the case would like to think this. If it had been used as a reason for future leniency, the Law would have ceased to have any force or meaning.

Chapter Seven

I have to break the chronological continuity I'd hoped to maintain so that I can complete my picture of Kenneth Diplock, and the effect he had on my life in the Temple.

My relationship with Theo Mathew had been at first that of a schoolboy to his headmaster, maturing with the years to that of a prefect to the headmaster, but I still kept a feeling of awe in his presence. With Diplock it was different. He was a few years younger than I and I had been in a position of some authority when he had come as a pupil, and although while practising in other chambers he had rapidly grown in stature as a lawyer, I still retained that first feeling of superiority when he asked to return to us. This diminished as I realised his genius and his capacity for intense hard work. It might have humbled me, but before it did our relationship developed into friendship, and when the bombs began to fall, and we shared the fears and dangers of the blitz together, a bond had been formed that could never be broken; afterwards I never felt that I was working for him, but in unison with him.

It was not long after the war that another great man joined our chambers, who was also to have a deep and lasting effect on my life; a man who differed greatly from both Theo and Kenneth. He was an explosive extrovert, a brilliant lawyer and an eloquent counsel in all types of work; unpredictable perhaps, but prepared and able at all times to form careful and reasoned opinions which were justified, if not always acceptable, in Law. He was also a man of high spirits, given at times to talking off the top of his head, which gave the impression to those who didn't, or hadn't tried, to know him, that he was making quick and unthinking decisions. It rarely happened in my experience, but I think this opinion in others prevented him from attaining the highest political office in the land. This man was Quintin Hogg.

In view of our contrasting temperaments it might be thought that Quintin and I would have quarrelled with each other. This was never true. With my sense of the theatre I believed I was able to recognise star quality when I saw it. I knew I could always count on Quintin to give an outstanding performance; it was my job to see that he had the right roles to play, where he could catch not only the public eye, but more important the eyes and ears of those who were prepared to provide good work and put up the money: I mean the clients. To reach this end I was ready to accept the temperamental behaviour that is expected from those who breathe a rarer atmosphere; that it was seldom forthcoming, and only when all reasonable argument had failed to achieve its purpose, I hope will help to lay the erroneously held opinion of Quintin Hogg that he was given to bouts of unreliability. Unreliability is not something that is acceptable at the Bar. Every thought, word and action has to be reasoned and controlled. It was the ability to do this that he took with him to both houses of parliament, and which was appreciated by those who worked near him. His occasional eccentricities, which were part of the whole man, were taken by some out of context and portrayed as absurdities.

I do not believe that you can split a man down the middle and, as was tried in Quintin's case, separate his political life from his life at the Bar. Many of the faculties and skills of the one are required by the other. He is the only barrister I know who has twice interrupted his legal career and, after long periods of absence, been able to re-establish himself. This to anyone connected with the Law speaks volumes; solicitors and clients do not like to brief barristers who are known to have outside interests, and can only be persuaded to do it when they are convinced that he is the best man for the job. Quintin was able so to convince them and this is again part of the measure of the man. That the leaders of the Conservative party were unable to give him similar recognition in 1963 was, I believe, not only a loss to the party, but an even greater one to the country.

I suppose that is the nearest I shall get to writing what can be taken as either a testimonial or a previous obituary of a great man. Later I shall, as I develop his story, show some of his warts, which again if taken out of context will be produced as evidence by his critics. It is a chance I shall have to take.

Quintin didn't come to our chambers until 1947, by which time the post-war reorganisation had taken place. I had given up the running of Bush James' chambers, but one of his barristers, Ifor Lloyd, asked if he could stay with us and was accepted, so that we maintained an interest in Divorce Law. Diplock had left the RAF and was now devoting all his considerable energies to the Law. Richard O'Sullivan, Carthew, Hubert Hull, Longland and H. A. Lincoln either joined, or returned, and a one-time pupil of Theo Mathew, James C. Leonard, came to us from Storey Dean's chambers at 3 Elm Court, next door to where I'd started in 1915. I believe I am right in saying that of Mathew's two hundred-odd pupils, James Leonard was his favourite, and in his will Theo left his Law Reports, and any possessions in his room at the Temple which he wanted, to him. Leonard was highly intelligent and humane. His practice was largely of Lawyer's Law; Civil and Commercial work. Eventually he became our leading junior, and to his delight took over Theo's room.

At this time young barristers returning from the war found accommodation difficult to come by, so I decided on an action which was unethical, and was frowned on by my superiors. Trustrum Eve, KC, whose services were required by the government, now wanted only a *pied-à-terre* in the Temple. I was able to negotiate with him so that I took three rooms in his chambers, paying the rent from my own pocket. In this way I was able to accommodate several young barristers. Some years later I was congratulated by my critics as this action helped to save our chamber in a time of crisis.

Since Quintin Hogg is the centre-piece of this chapter, I must once again turn back the clock. He came as a pupil to Theo

Mathew in 1932. Some weeks previously I received a visit from his father, Lord Hailsham, at that time an ex-Lord Chancellor, an office he was to resume in 1935. Over the years I had known him as Douglas Hogg, a junior when I first went to the Temple who had taken Silk in 1917, and was one of the only four KCs created during the whole period of the First World War. He was certainly one of the most successful barristers of his time; this is demonstrated by his earnings at the Bar, which rose to a height that has seldom been equalled in money value. Between May 1920 and April 1921 his income was £40,933, and in the following year, £46,541. What makes these figures even more extraordinary is that most of the fees marked on the briefs were for comparatively small sums, and came from an exceptionally wide range of solicitors.

Most barristers, however, attach greater importance to the esteem of office than to hard cash, for in later years, as Lord Hailsham, he remarked, 'At the Bar I made £40,000 a year; as a Law Officer, £20,000; as Lord Chancellor, £10,000, and at present as Lord President of the Council, £5,000.' Similar diminutions were to affect Quintin's income. In what has become an acquisitive world, and one in which lawyers are often accused of fleecing the public, barristers, generally speaking, cannot be considered as being guilty.

My only contact with Lord Hailsham over the years had been to pass the time of day with him whenever we met; though I suppose he had noticed the change in my fortunes, just as I had followed his. Our paths, however, had not crossed on legal matters. It was with some surprise therefore that I greeted him when he came into our chambers. I imagined that he had come to see Theo. 'No, it's you I want to see, Sydney,' he said. 'Mr Mathew has told me that he will take my son Quintin as a pupil if you agree, so I'm here to get your approval.' Needless to say, I didn't hesitate in giving it. 'Good', he replied, 'I understand your principals have a high regard for your work, and I'm sure Quintin will benefit from being under your wing.' Then he produced a cheque book. 'I believe the fees are a 100 guineas for the pupillage?' I agreed the figure and he made out the cheque. As he handed it to me he said, 'You'll look after my boy, won't you Sydney?' I told him I would do my best for him. When he left the chambers I glanced at the cheque; it was for 110 guineas. I took it as it was meant; a kindly gesture. I think if he had given me a separate cheque for the extra guineas I would have had it framed, and kept it till today.

When I put it around the Temple that young Hogg was joining us, my news got a mixed reception. All agreed that academically and intellectually he was brilliant, indeed there was no denying this: a scholar at Eton and later at Christ Church, Oxford, a first in Greats, and a Fellow of All Souls' College; he had also been President of the Oxford Union, so all told he couldn't have done much better than that. But there were those who tried to knock him; remarks such as, 'Conceited and arrogant,' 'Too clever by half,' were bandied around, so I was a little concerned as to what to expect. In the event I was not disappointed.

By now I was accustomed to the behaviour of young men of his class and distinction. Youth at that time was very sure of itself. It had cause to be. The British Empire was larger, if not greater, than it had ever been, the war had decimated a young generation and another had now emerged, which felt its destiny was to fill the gap, and it had every confidence that it would be able to succeed, and to succeed well. The old order of things still prevailed; the General Strike had collapsed, and opportunities were there for the taking for the upper middle classes. Quintin Hogg was one of that generation though with a difference; he was an intellectual. This put him outside the pack. For some reason in a country that pretends to care so much for education, we despise those who accept the opportunities offered them, and take them as far as they are able. Perhaps in his earlier years, Quintin was inclined to flaunt his intellect. He most certainly suffered fools, or people he considered fools, badly. He was also thought overcritical, though I would prefer to call it challenging. He was unable to accept any dictum or tradition without first submitting it to close examination. All in all, therefore, he was a man who, while he took some understanding, responded to those who were

125

prepared to make the effort.

These, of course, are some of my opinions of the young man as I knew him, but given with hindsight. They were not those that came to me when a tousle-haired, fresh-faced, ungainly figure first appeared in our chambers. It may seem impertinent that someone with my poor schooling and ordinary background should pass opinion and judgement on someone whose mind and potential were so considerably superior to my own. That's as may be; I can only say that, as a result of my contact over the years with fine minds, something must have brushed off on to me so that as I grew older I was able to judge quality, even if I was not able to copy it. It was my job to try to determine the worth of those barristers who were, or were likely to be, in my hands. Quintin was such a one, when at the age of twenty-five he came to us.

Strangely, unlike Diplock who had preceded him by a year, he didn't get on terms with Theo Mathew. He found him at first a bit crochety, soaked in the traditions of the Bar, and in comparison with the dons he had mixed with at Oxford, not a particularly good teacher. It may have been that temperamentally at that time they were miles apart. However, despite his opinions Quintin worked hard for Theo. He was, as I've said, academically gifted, and he was also intensely ambitious and competitive by nature; a slave to his work, though occasionally careless because of the speed at which he worked. He was most anxious to be in court. He enjoyed fighting cases. I was able to satisfy his appetite by putting devilling in his way, and my old friend Packer also fed him plenty. He was first and foremost an advocate at that time, practising the art which he had learned at the Oxford Union. But he wasn't primarily interested in criminal work; he determined to acquire a knowledge of civil law, which when he went into practice he was able to develop, and as early as 1935 he had published a book on the Law of Arbitration.

He left us to go to Eric Sachs, later a Lord Justice, whose chambers were upstairs in Number 4, so I saw him regularly and naturally followed his progress with interest. It was about 1936 that I heard, or read, that he was trying to get himself adopted as a prospective Conservative candidate. Strangely, despite both his

126

obvious suitability and his parentage, he didn't find it easy and it wasn't until 1938, with the death of Robert Bourne, the Tory member for Oxford City, that he was given the opportunity of fighting a by-election. He won, but had hardly settled in the House before war was declared. He joined up straight away and was commissioned into the Rifle Brigade. In 1941 he was posted to the Middle East where he joined their 2nd battalion. He called into his chambers a few days before embarking. I met him as I was leaving for lunch. 'Hello, Sydney,' he called. 'It's also goodbye. I'm off to the wars. The next time you hear of me I shall probably be lying in a six foot by four foot grave in some foreign land.' He said it cheerfully, and meant it as a joke, but it spoiled my meal for me. I was always superstitious. Fortunately my ill omens proved wrong, and I saw him again in 1942, when because of an illness he had been down-graded and returned home.

There's no doubt that he could quite legitimately have worked his ticket and returned to the Bar. He didn't; he confined his extra-military duties to politics. He felt it would be taking an unfair advantage of other barristers still in the Services if he started practising again.

When the war was over he returned to his old chambers. It was some time in 1947 when he visited me. 'Look, Sydney,' he said, 'I seem to be getting nowhere; the work just isn't coming my way; do you think there's any chance of you finding a room for me?' I told I couldn't hold out any great hopes, but promised to see what I could do. 'I'm not too worried about a room, I just want my name on the door, then you can let everyone know that I'm alive and that I'm back at the Bar.' I wanted him with us but despite what he said I had to find him some accommodation. As it happened there was one small room about twelve foot by six foot which no one wanted, so on that same day, I offered it to him. He accepted immediately, the following week his name went up, and within two days of joining us, I had him in court. From that moment he never looked back.

At first I was able to give him work which Diplock, Hull, and to a lesser extent, O'Sullivan, couldn't cope with, but it quickly came to him in his own right.

He was briefed in a number of personal injury cases and was successful in getting clients awarded large sums in compensation. This caused considerable concern among Insurance Companies with the result that the policy of 'If you can't beat them, join them' meant that he was quickly asked to appear for them, and was able to stand with his feet on both sides of the fence. He was also found to be particularly able to persuade justices to grant licences for the sale of alcoholic liquor so that as the bigger stores moved into this lucrative business he was in constant demand.

His almost mercurial success was not only due to his brilliance at Law; I think as a result of his war experiences his manner had become more human. He now had the common touch which, coupled with his intense loyalty and dependability, helped widen his range of clients. There were occasional bouts of irascibility, and when these occurred he would take it out on whoever was around, and since I was in the front rank I was generally the whipping boy. After a time there was also a whipping girl, for he engaged as a personal secretary Miss Deidre Shannon, or Shannie as we all called her. She was a beautiful girl, a doctor's daughter and as efficient as she was attractive. She was able quickly to adapt herself to legal work, but although she had a deep affection and admiration for Quintin, she found it difficult to come to terms with his temperament and moods. Many's the time I had to hand her my handkerchief so that she could stem the tears of indignation that Quintin's abrupt rebuke or criticism brought to her eyes. I tried to explain to her that his words had little depth, and that his gibes were forgotten as soon as made, but made things no better. Then one day he called me into his room and delivered a broadside at me. I came out in a flaming temper and I picked up my bowler hat, threw it on the floor and stamped up and down on it in a frenzy. While I was engaged in this war dance, Quintin came out of his office to see what was disturbing the peace. He stood there and began roaring with laughter, which was quickly taken up by Shannie, and, when I stopped, looked and listened to them, I too saw the funny side and joined in the hilarity. Suddenly Quintin pointed at Shannie. 'Look, Sydney,' he exclaimed, 'you've done it now; you've made her cry,' and as he turned back towards his room he muttered, 'There's no understanding of women.' From that day Shannie's attitude towards him underwent a marked change, and her tears became a rarity.

If ever Quintin felt he had behaved unreasonably towards us, he had his own way of apologising. The day after he would come to the chambers and say, 'I had a wretched attack of the stomach ache yesterday; however, I took some medicine last night and I'm as right as rain again today.' He'd then beam at us, and go on to his room. We also knew from the moment he came in which way any of his cases had gone. If the verdict had been in his favour he would bustle in wreathed in smiles, and settle down equably and easily. If it went against him, he would burst through the door and bark, 'Today there has been a grave miscarriage of justice,' and we would look forward to the rest of the day with some apprehension. There were times when we had to take the law into our own hands. Whenever he felt he had been personally affronted, or ill-used by a judge he reacted oversensitively; he would call Shannie in, dictate an irate letter, sign it and tell her to see that it was posted immediately. We soon discovered that it was no use protesting there and then, or trying to explain that such an action could jeopardize judges' future attitudes, so with Shannie's co-operation, I devised a means of temporarily delaying them. One evening she showed me a particularly blunt and outspoken letter. 'I'm sure this should never be sent, Sydney,' she said, 'not at any rate in its present form.' This gave me an idea. 'Hold it up until tomorrow, show it him in the morning and say we both thought he would like to rephrase the second paragraph.' We were taking our lives into our own hands, but I thought it might well be worth it. I was right, the ploy worked perfectly. When Shannie presented it for possible correction, he quickly read it through and said, 'I don't know what I was thinking about, writing a letter like this. It doesn't need rewording, it wants destroying,' and he screwed it up and threw it into the waste paper basket. From that time on, when in doubt we employed the same method. I believe that eventually Quintin realised what we were doing, for sometimes he would forestall us when he came into chambers by saying, 'Did you send that letter I dictated last night?' and when we said we hadn't, he'd reply, 'Good, because I've had second thoughts about it; I don't think it should go after all.' In a way these letters were a kind of therapy, for through them he was able quickly to get rid of his irritation, and despite the extra work, it provided another source of amusement to our lives.

Punctuality was something he both practised himself and demanded of others. Only once did I know him to be really late, and this was for a purpose. He had several times been kept waiting by a particular judge, and he determined to get his own back. The court assembled and the judge called on Lord Hailsham. He was not there. When the judge asked where he was we could only say we didn't know. 'Well, we can't begin without him, so I suppose we shall have to wait,' was the disgruntled reply. He could have adjourned, but decided to sit it out. It was half an hour before Quintin appeared, and his lordship had grown more aggrieved as each minute had passed. 'Where have you been?' he demanded. Quintin simply replied by apologising to his lordship and the court. Again the judge pressed him for his excuse. 'I have no excuse, I can only offer my humblest apologies,' was the reply, and so it went on with Quintin refusing to explain or offer reason. Eventually the exasperated judge gave up and the case began. Afterwards I asked Quintin why he had made no effort to account for his absence. 'To begin with whatever I had said would have been a lie, secondly it would have given the judge a bone to worry and he would have been able to castigate me. As it was he had to eventually accept my apology and demean himself by doing it with a bad grace.'

On the death of his father, in August 1950, Quintin succeeded him as the second Viscount Hailsham. Despite the fact that he had been an invalid for some considerable time, his father's death must have been the cause of deep sorrow, for he lost a great friend and adviser. I don't know to what extent Quintin mirrored himself on his father but a shared quality, and one which I think was the cornerstone of Quintin's character, was their absolute loyalty both to family, friends and the Conservative party. It was something that spilled over into his career at the Bar. Judges and barristers might have had cause occasionally to criticise his quixotic behaviour, but never did I hear a whisper of reproach concerning his personal dealings with anyone, either friend or opponent. He never to my knowledge let anyone down. It was the same in chambers. He made no decisions that were likely to affect us as a unit, without first consulting me; and that included his acceptance or rejection of his political appointments. Together we would discuss the pros and cons of the situation, he would explain how his possible actions could affect his legal work, and then ask for my opinion. I am not saying that he necessarily took advice, but when he didn't he gave satisfactory and acceptable reasons for not doing so.

With his succession to his father's title, Quintin had to surrender his seat in the House of Commons. Although he resented this, I was over the moon with delight. Now we could work without thinking about division bells, debates, political meetings and the like. With Kenneth Diplock leading the field, an international lawyer travelling the world, his services in constant demand by clients who could afford him, with Quintin sprinting fast, and my stable full of other thoroughbreds who were more than earning their keep, I felt I must be the leading trainer in the Temple Stakes!

My life settled into a happy and rewarding routine. It was never dull or predictable; even after thirty-five years at the Temple I could not anticipate what any day would bring. I was now financially well off, and by the standards of my early background, I was wealthy. My earnings during this time were around £10,000 a year, and rising. It had not been easy for me to adjust myself to this kind of income. It had increased year by year, but apart from sending my daughter Carol-Anne away to school, running a car, making my wife Do understand she could now choose whatever clothes she wanted, and always sitting in the best seats on our regular visits to the theatre, my life style was much the same as it had been when I first married. So after the Chancellor of the Exchequer had had his share, I was able regularly to invest quite substantial amounts.

I had become interested in photography, and it was this hobby that in 1953 was to give me a real involvement in the world of the theatre. I was experimenting in colour photography, which at that time was in its infancy. There was a little man off the Tottenham Court Road who did my developing and printing, and advised me generally on techniques. One morning around eleven, I went to see him to collect some pictures. I was told by his assistant that he was out having coffee with a young lady but was expected back shortly, so would I wait. Within a matter of minutes he returned with this young lady. As he showed her into the room I rose, to find myself gazing into a mammoth bosom. Now my particular fetish had always been the forearm, but no man could but he mesmerised by these glorious mammary glands. Eventually I tore my eyes away and glanced up at their owner. I was surprised to see so young and innocent a face above such a fabulous property development. 'Oh Sydney, I'm glad you're here, it may be most fortuitous,' said Harry, my photographic friend. 'Now let me introduce you. This is Miss Norma Sykes, this is Mr Sydney Aylett.' I stood back, put out my hand and made some formal noises. I was a bit concerned with Harry's remark that it was fortuitous that I was there, for I wondered of what possible assistance a middle-aged barristers' clerk could be to such a young lady. 'Miss Sykes,' he continued, 'has come to London from Blackpool to try and find employment in the theatre, and knowing your keen interest in show business I thought perhaps you could give her the benefit of your advice.' Without any hesitation I replied, 'My advice to you, young lady, is to get on the next train and go back home.' 'That's just what I told her, but she's very obstinate, and says she won't,' said Harry. Miss Sykes echoed his last words. 'Well sit down there for a moment,' he pointed to a chair, 'while I take Mr Aylett through and show him his pictures.' I followed him into his office. 'What are you trying to get me into,' I whispered, 'and where on earth did you find her?' 'She came in here thinking I was a photographer, she wanted some pictures taken for agents. After I'd explained that I only did the developing and printing she started pouring her heart out to me about this stage business, so I took her out for a cup of coffee and tried to make her see sense and go back home. Then knowing you were coming round I brought her back here to meet you thinking you might be able to help in some way.' 'Where is she staying?' I asked. 'One of those hotels in the King's Cross area.' 'Oh my God,' I responded, knowing what that could mean. 'Exactly, Sydney, so we've got to do something.' 'What do you suggest?' I asked. 'Well, why don't you take her out for lunch, listen to her story, tell her what a wicked place London is for a girl like her and try and get her to go back. You're just the man for the job with your legal background.' 'If I tell her what a wicked place this is, she'll probably want to stay. I'm certain I'll do more harm than good,' I said, trying to wriggle out of the situation. 'Now look, Sydney,' Harry went on, 'if you don't try and do something for the girl she'll be on your conscience for the rest of your life.' I didn't see it that way. 'What about your conscience, it was you that found her,' I retorted. 'Look, we're getting nowhere, will you or won't you?' I was cornered. 'All right, I'll take her out to lunch, but if she's obstinate I'll bring her back to you.' So a compromise was reached. I was no Sir Galahad, and was certain that I would be returning her within an hour.

Norma seemed pleased that I'd taken her over, and she babbled away as we walked to Lyons Corner House, the large restaurant on the corner of Tottenham Court Road and Oxford Street. I chose it because of its size. I didn't fancy being caught in a *tête à tête* in some intimate Soho restaurant by any of my legal acquaintances. As we walked along I found I was only half listening to her chatter; I had become conscious of the attention Norma was attracting from passers-by. It seemed that every man's head turned towards her and from the looks in their eyes, which ranged from admiration to downright lechery, it became apparent to me that she had something. It wasn't just the bosom; she radiated a sort of sensual purity, which sounds like a contradiction in terms, but I think she gave a different kind of sensation to everyone who saw her. She was what I suppose is meant by the term sex symbol. It was the same in the restaurant; she seemed to hypnotize, and I noticed there were several kicks under the table from ladies with

133

male escorts. Eventually I was able to get her full story. She had been born in Lancashire, and her mother and father now kept a boarding house in Blackpool. On and off she'd recently spent several months in hospitals with a leg infection, and a series of operations had left a scar which she said prevented her from using beauty contests as a means of getting into the theatre. Her illness had also affected her education; she had received very little schooling, indeed she was the classic example of 'a dumb blonde'. 'How do you propose keeping yourself while you look for work in the theatre?' I asked. 'I thought perhaps I could be a waitress, something of that kind, somewhere where I could get time off to go for auditions.' I explained that employers expected regular hours from their workers. 'I can make necklaces with beads, they taught me that in hospital,' she volunteered. I could see I was getting nowhere. 'Exactly what do your parents think of it all?' I asked. 'They say the same as you, but I'm not going back, I'm sure I will find someone who will help me,' she said. It was a sort of blackmail. But I was no sugar daddy. Even if I'd been tempted, I'd seen too often in the courts what happened to those who trod that primrose path. But still her magnetism fascinated me, and the effect on others around gave me to think that perhaps I might be able to do something for her. To be honest it wasn't altruism. If she did succeed, it would bring me into closer contact with the world I loved, and there would be the glamorous kickback of having discovered a star. In a way it reflected my work at the Bar, though without the financial rewards, for I was determined that my motives would never be found to be other than the highest.

'Do you think it possible for me to meet your parents? Could you persuade them to come to London? If they agree, there is a plan I could put into operation, but I'm doing nothing without their consent.' Norma thought for a few seconds, 'I'll ring them tonight. I don't know about Dad, he's none too well, but I'm sure Mum will, anyway I'll do my best to get her here.' It was agreed that she would phone me and let me know what was happening, and after I'd delivered a few well-chosen words about the perils of the big city, we parted.

The following day I had a call from her saying that her mother

134

had agreed to come to London, and could we meet somewhere the day after. I suggested the Regent Palace Hotel, since it was a place that anyone who didn't know London could easily find. I now decided I'd better explain to Do what was happening. It wasn't easy. It's strange how disingenuous the most honourable motives can sound when you try putting them to your wife. Her first reaction didn't help, 'Sounds a peculiar kind of brief to me; what fee is marked on it?' However, I hadn't worked for barristers for nothing. I pulled out my oratorical stops, compared Norma to our own daughter and with the promise that I would introduce them should it be decided that Norma would stay on in London to try her luck, I think I succeeded in convincing Do that I had done the only thing possible under the circumstances.

The meeting with Mrs Sykes went well. She was a jolly woman, and seemed grateful for my interest in her daughter. I then explained my plan, though I had some difficulty in expressing myself delicately. I said that I had noticed that in America the big bosom had become big business; I mentioned the names of Jane Russell, Jayne Mansfield and Marilyn Monroe. Mrs Sykes took my point, albeit a little rustically. 'Aye, I see what you mean,' she broke in, 'and our Norma's got a couple of beauties, hasn't she? I expect she has told you her measurements, she's forty-one inches round the tits, and she's got an eighteen-inch waist,' she said proudly. I noticed Norma's eyes flickering modestly. I recovered my equilibrium, and went on to say that while it might prove difficult at this stage to get theatre work, she could well break into the modelling world. I told her that I knew an agent, Bill Watts, who specialised in models and also groomed young starlets, and that I could introduce Norma to him and to Noel Maine, a camera man for Baron the Court photographer. I explained that I had one or two other contacts we could try if those two failed. We agreed that if after a month Norma seemed to be getting nowhere, she would return home; and finally I explained that she would have to live in a more salubrious neighbourhood than the King's Cross area. 'Well I'm sure we're both very grateful to you, judge,' Mrs Sykes said, when I'd outlined my plan. 'Ee you don't mind me calling you that, do you?' she went on, and she hugged me close to her own ample bosom. 'It's more friendly, and you did sound a bit like a judge delivering your verdict on our Norma.' So 'the judge' I was to be to the members of the family from then on.

As I'd promised I made the suggested introductions and to my delight Norma was most favourably received. Noel Maine found her photogenic, and said he was sure he'd be able to use her for fashion modelling. He wasn't worried about the scar on her leg, his interests were on a higher plane. Bill Watts was as enthusiastic but was concerned about her name. 'It won't do at all, she sounds like some relation of that unwholesome fellow in *Oliver Twist*. We must think of something else.' I'm not sure which one of us had the idea, but there was a show running in London at the time called *Sabrina Fair*, and it was decided then and there that Sabrina was the name of our blonde bombshell.

Inevitably there followed a short period of inactivity, and Norma became depressed; but Bill Watts had made me promise not to show her to anyone else until he had exhausted all his contacts. Then came the breakthrough. BBC Television was producing a new series with the comedian Arthur Askey, 'Big Hearted Arthur,' and they wanted a young, plentifully-endowed blonde for him to fence around. Bill Watts was asked to send about a dozen for camera tests, and said he would include Sabrina if she wanted to compete. She did, and won by several inches. The extraordinary thing was that she hadn't to speak a single word, she just had to stand there and react to the antics of the funny little man. Considerable play of course was made of her figure, but Norma was now fully accustomed to this and was quite unperturbed with Arthur Askey bobbing around her boobs. The great British public weren't. They went mad over this silent siren, and the press responded accordingly. *Picture Post*, an illustrated magazine with a readership of millions, quickly had a picture of her on their cover, and offers began to pour in for photographic sessions and personal appearances, and with the offers came money. Sabrina had arrived. So had the bosom. Bigger and better falsies were demanded and fashions changed. Norma also changed, and changed fast, though she still behaved towards me as she had when we first met. She regarded me as her business manager, protector from the men who now began to besiege her, and eventually as her legal adviser. I discovered that this seemingly naive girl was in fact as sharp as a needle. I mentioned to her that an article about her was possibly libellous. She was on to it with her claws. It was settled out of court, and she received a generous sum in damages. From that time on she scanned the papers, not for the nice things they said about her, but to explore the legal possibilities of the nasty things. She had no belief in the saying that there's no such thing as bad publicity; at one time she had eleven law suits on the go; of these seven reached the setting-down stage, and appeared in the case lists. Naturally they were handled by my barristers, so that although I received no direct money for the services I rendered her, I did collect in another way. I also found it ironic that I, who had devoted my life to placing men with the powers of oratory, should have been partly responsible for the success of someone who was always required to keep her mouth shut.

She travelled the world to display her charms. She was to have appeared in the Command Performance before the Queen in 1956, but to her great disappointment it was cancelled because of the Suez crisis. While she was in America, some humorist issued a challenge to Sabrina and Jayne Mansfield, to be measured on stage to prove whose bust was the greater. Sabrina accepted readily, but Miss Mansfield would have none of it, so yet another of the world's great secrets has never been unfolded.

Although Sabrina was a regular visitor to Number 4 Paper Buildings, only once did she and Quintin confront each other. He mistook her for a temporary typist I had engaged. I hastily tried to put matters right by explaining who she was. It was obvious that she meant nothing in Quintin's life, so for once fumbling for something to say, he asked her if she was married. 'Not yet,' replied Norma, 'but I shall be in a few weeks time – to an American gynaecologist.' 'I'm sure, my dear, you could find no more suitable a husband,' he remarked, as he gazed down at her. She did marry her gynaecologist. Do and I received an invitation to the wedding (Do, by the way, had quickly come to terms with our relationship when she had met her); we didn't go since they were married in America, but I continued to correspond with her. One of her later letters confirmed that old adage that nothing lasts forever, for in it Norma informed me that her famous forty-one inch bust had diminished to such a degree that she had been mistaken for Twiggy.

My excursion into the theatre proved a pleasant diversion. It didn't pass my colleagues unnoticed, and a certain amount of friendly banter rippled round the Temple and its precincts. One or two less kind people suggested that I would have made a better theatrical agent than a barristers' clerk, but they were those who were casting envious eyes on our chambers. But it was to help me in my real work, too. Up until the time I met Norma, when I was entertaining clients (and by clients I mean solicitors clerks and their like) I had confined myself to the more humble eating and drinking establishments. When meeting her friends I had opened the doors of the Ritz, the Savoy, the Dorchester; I had eaten in the better Soho restaurants, and I'd discovered that while they were a little more expensive then those I had used previously, for the comfort and entertainment they offered they were worth it, and that anyway they were now well within reach of my purse. It had been a new world to me, and it was most certainly a new one to my clients. They were impressed, particularly when I was able to point out some celebrity, and were more willing to consider fees on the highest levels. Tea at the Ritz I found was at that time almost the cheapest meal in London. Other people later recognised this, and the price had to rise to protect the hotel from invasion. So all-in-all my encounter with Sabrina proved an amusing and not unrewarding experience.

It was in 1953, the year I met Sabrina, that Quintin took Silk; Diplock had been appointed a King's Counsellor some years before. For both the sometimes dangerous transition from junior to leader had been easy, successful and rewarding. The seniority of Diplock as a Silk does not imply that he was a better lawyer than Quintin. I once, rather foolishly, voiced such an opinion to Kenneth, saying that I thought he had the more brilliant mind. I received a quick rebuke, 'Such a comparison cannot be made. If it

138

was possible to equate us, you might say that while I have concentrated my energies on the Law, Quintin has spread his talents widely and to the greater benefit of mankind.' In my own defence I must say that when I told Quintin recently what I had said, and Diplock's reply, he, to a degree, justified my statement, 'I consider Diplock to be one of the two finest Law Lords of the time.' He did name the other, but I think in fairness this should remain a matter of speculation.

Both Quintin and Kenneth continued to enhance the reputation of our chambers, and I could strut around the Temple and smirk with a deal of pride at both their and my achievements. However, at the age of fifty-five I was to experience what I had preached, that there is only one thing certain about success – that it has to end. I suppose I should have foreseen what was to come. I had been warned early on by Packer, and I'd watched the same thing happen to other chambers. It was just before Christmas 1955 that I received a message from the Lord Chancellor's office, saying that the Chancellor, Lord Kilmuir, whom I had known well over the years as David Maxwell Fyfe, wished to see Kenneth Diplock that same day at the House, and that the matter was of some urgency. I immediately sensed what was afoot. A High Court judge had recently retired, Kenneth was to be offered the job and if he accepted he would be lost to our chambers forever. If he accepted it. I tried to remember whether it was a situation we had ever discussed. For him it would mean a big drop in income, but then he had never seemed concerned about money. It would also mean isolation from many of his colleagues at the Bar, a great deal of night work in preparing 'reserved judgements', of travelling and sleeping in judge's lodgings, some of which were not particularly comfortable. For some the disadvantages would have outweighed the honour, but the more I thought of it the more certain I was that Kenneth would accept; and I was correct. To a man of his kind it was the fulfilment of a life devoted to the Law. He could now use the knowledge and experience he had gained over the years to uphold the principles he so firmly believed in. He was a comparatively young man, and while his immediate preferment was sufficient for him to think about for the moment,

139

he must have known that it was the first step on a new ladder. So it proved to be, for he became a Lord Justice in the Court of Appeal, and later, in the House of Lords, a Lord of Appeal-in-Ordinary, which apart from the office of Lord Chancellor (one he could not hope to obtain as he had no involvement in politics) is the highest judicial appointment in the land.

When Kenneth told me of the invitation and his decision, I naturally swallowed my own feelings and congratulated him on the honour that had been conferred upon him. There was a lot of work to be done disposing of his impending cases, since he was required to take up his new office in a few weeks. 'You'll sit in on a few of my cases from time to time, won't you Sydney? I shall rely on you to tell me if I am suffering from "benchitis".'

I was anxious to discover whether Kenneth had been the Chancellor's first choice. As I've inferred it was not unheard of for senior counsel to reject preferment, and an appointment could be made from a third, or even a fourth choice. I was able to discover that this had not been the case with Kenneth. Lord Kilmuir had indeed written to Lord Goddard asking for his opinion. Goddard had replied with a brief note saying, 'I propose Edmund Davies,' to which Lord Kilmuir, equally brief, answered, 'I choose Kenneth Diplock.' Goddard, though, was not far short of the mark, for Edmund Davies was made a high court judge soon afterwards, and, following in Diplock's footsteps, later went to the Court of Appeal and to the Lords. I think I'm right in saying that, at the time, Davies was the only judge able to conduct a trial in the Welsh language.

There was one consolation for me over Diplock's departure, and that was that I did not have to go with him as his clerk. This is not as churlish as it sounds, for the reduction in income would have been near disastrous for me. Judge's clerks had for some years been classed as Civil Service appointments, and it was no longer the practice for a chief clerk to remain with his head of chambers on his elevation to the Bench. Also, when I'd got over my initial disappointment I felt more secure in the knowledge that I still had Quintin, who had now taken over as head of chambers, and that he would continue to be with us until he followed Kenneth to the Bench. After all, I thought, his succession to the title had ruled out any further political involvement, or so I, and I think he himself, believed. How wrong we both were. Hardly had I reorganised the chambers, when Quintin confronted me with the news that he had been asked by Sir Anthony Eden, then Prime Minister, if he would succeed Lord Cilcennin, who was to resign in the spring of 1956, as First Lord of the Admiralty. Quintin sought my opinion. What could I say? It was a job that one of his heroes, Winston Churchill, had once held, and although at this moment there was no immediate possibility of it leading to the premiership, who could tell what the future might bring. It was all the more agonizing for me because only six weeks before he had told me that Lord Salisbury, the leader of the House of Lords, had on the authorization of the Prime Minister offered him the position of Postmaster-General, an unimportant office which he had had no hesitation in turning down on the spot. So since then I had thought we were clear of further political interference. I think I probably showed my own disappointment and my concern for our chambers. He comforted me somewhat by saying that, if he did decide to take it, he would only be away until the next general election, which he calculated correctly would be in 1959, but which he predicted incorrectly the Labour Party would win.

He did of course accept the appointment, but there was a period in limbo during which my hopes rose. He was supposed to have taken office in the spring, but as the weeks went by and there was still no announcement of Cilcennin's resignation, Quintin continued to work at the Bar and I began to wonder if the whole thing was just a pipe dream. Then the papers got hold of the story of his impending appointment. This put the cat amongst the pigeons as far as his legal practice was concerned, and I found myself in every kind of embarrassing position trying to answer clients' questions about his future movements. Not unnaturally, Quintin was tetchy, and wretched about the position he and I had been placed in. I later found out the cause. The Khrushchev–Bulganin visit to Britain took place in the early summer, and while they were over here a Commander Crabb was discovered exploring the bottom of a Russian cruiser. The Admiralty was involved, and Cilcennin refused to resign as he felt that to do so would be to admit his personal responsibility and that it would be interpreted as his disgrace. Eventually Quintin sorted things out, though at one moment it was touch and go as to whether he would reconsider his position and continue in chambers. He eventually went to the Admiralty in September 1956.

Before he left he made one particular effort to help save the status of our chambers. He wrote to Sir Hartley Shawcross, who had been the Attorney General in Attlee's government. He had heard that my old friend Matthew Robinson, Sir Hartley's chief clerk, had recently died and thought that Sir Hartley would now like to come to our chambers to be looked after by me. I was shown his reply, which said that had he been continuing to practise at the Bar, he most certainly would have accepted, but that he had decided to give up his legal career in favour of the City. So another straw was snatched from my fingers. As if things were not bad enough, two other barristers, Ifor Lloyd and A. H. (Hereward) Ormerod decided to leave around this time. So when I surveyed the wreckage I found I was left with James Leonard, who became head of chambers, and the 'boys' I housed in the rooms I had taken over from Trustrum Eve. Was I glad of my post-war opportunism now!

How we survived those next three or four years I shall never know. Much of the credit must be given to James Leonard for his patient guiding hands, but I think that without too much conceit I can claim my share. While over the years my jaunty attitude and appearance and my more than life-size behaviour had earned me the reputation of being a bit of a card, it had not damaged the opinion of solicitors that I was knowledgeable in the ways of the Law and the abilities of barristers, that I knew in what branches they specialised, that I was not over-greedy in negotiating fees, and that above all I was reliable. They also remembered that I had been able to help them out of difficulties in the past. One old friend, who was an ever present help in trouble, was Eric Fletcher, senior partner in the firm of Denton, Hall & Burgin, who had been the Labour Deputy Speaker in the House of

Commons, and was later to become Lord Fletcher. He had handled a lot of Diplock's work, and still continued to feed me with everything he could. Another was Herbert Baron, for whom Quintin did much of his Insurance work. He continued to pass whatever he could in the direction of Number 4. There were many others too, who, when they saw that I was in need, put anything they could my way. This was very useful to the 'boys'. A lot of it was 'bits and pieces' – a phrase I'd adopted during the halcyon days as a term of derision, but these were now briefs that I was very glad to lay my hands on.

One of my older 'boys' was Maurice Drake, a pupil of James Leonard, who quickly became a very useful junior and eventually built up a good general practice, finally taking Silk and becoming head of chambers. His recent appointment as a Judge of the High Court, Queen's Bench Division, has particularly delighted me as it made a judicial grandfather of our chambers; for Maurice was a pupil of Judge Leonard, himself a pupil of Theo Mathew. Others were Robin McEwan, a great friend of the Royals, who left the Bar in 1960; Helen Shore who later married Sir Delves Borough-ton, Baronet; she was a talented lawyer who was just too beauti-ful and enchanting to have been left alone to make a career at the Bar; Charles Monteith, an outstanding scholar and Fellow of All Souls, who was probably more brilliant academically than the rest of my 'boys' put together but who didn't go down too well in places like the Clerkenwell Police Court or County Courts, which were all I could offer him in those days, so he retired and made a career in publishing; Anthony Lincoln, who again left us around 1959 to go into Commercial chambers, and Roland Brown who became a successful junior, leaving us in 1961 to become Attorney General to Tanganyika (now Tanzania).

Mention of Roland Brown reminds me of a case in which he was concerned. I particularly remember it because it created a situation whereby I met and lost my heart to the Labour Shadow Minister, Barbara Castle. It was with some trepidation that I heard she was visiting our chambers; her reputation was that of a fire-brand, an Amazon who ate people like me for breakfast. She was to see Roland about an action she was bringing against the television broadcaster, Christopher Chataway. To my delight and astonishment I met a charming, attractive, soft-spoken redhead, with whom I had hardly exchanged two or three words before I realised that I adored her.

Unfortunately for Barbara, her case floundered. She had made the mistake of taking her parliamentary colleagues' advice on legal matters, and of keeping the case within the party. She first consulted the Shadow Attorney General Lynn Ungoed-Thomas, QC, who immediately and sensibly admitted that he was a Chancery man and knew nothing about libel. She then went to another Labour party QC who should have told her that he had never done a defamation case in his life. He didn't, and accepted the brief, handing it to Roland Brown to do the pleading. There's no doubt that Roland did this beautifully, but a week before the trial he accepted the appointment in Tanzania, and Maurice Drake stepped in as junior. From the moment our leader opened his mouth at the trial, his inexperience in such a case showed itself not only to the judge and the opposition, but also to Mrs Castle. At lunch on the first day she asked Maurice point blank if he had ever led before in a defamation case. Maurice quickly stuffed some food into his mouth and made some indistinguishable noises, but Barbara wasn't fooled and my sweet, adorable lady became a wild cat. My affection turned to admiration. She couldn't be bamboozled or cajoled, and her criticisms were bang on the nail. She realised that Maurice was in no way to blame, but that didn't help him, he still had to take a lot of the punishment. The case was of course duly lost, but things didn't stop there as far as I was concerned, for when it came to the gathering in of fees, Mrs Castle seemed to think that because it was a political matter, we would accept heavy cuts as a contribution towards the Labour movement. I explained that in matters which concerned money, I had no political allegiance. It seemed to me a rational enough statement, but it was unacceptable. I had to give ground, which after forty-five years' service was unprecedented. I saw to it that it was kept a secret, both from colleagues and clients. In fact today it makes me feel ashamed as I write about it, and I only do so to point what I think is the moral of this case. 'Always go to the disinterested professionals for advice.'

So the dangerous years passed. I prayed for a Labour victory in the general election of 1959, but my prayers went unanswered. By then though things had improved; both Drake and Lincoln had built up good junior practices. I hoped that James Leonard would take Silk. I was quite certain that he was someone who would have benefited by doing so, and for me to say that means something, for I was always over-cautious in recommending such a step. Recently I was reminded by Maurice Drake of the time when he was a pupil and I walked into the Dog Hole and announced to the 'boys' that I had just seen a barrister cut his throat. 'Good God, what did you do about it?' was the universal horrified response. 'There was nothing I could do,' I said. 'I tried to stop him, but he has insisted on applying for Silk.' I was right in my prognostication; from being a successful junior, he became an unsuccessful KC. This though would never have happened to Leonard. Perhaps he decided to follow his great friend Theo Mathew's example. Only he knows.

Towards the end of the 1950s two established barristers joined us, Gordon Friend and Langton Davies. Friend was most rightly named, for a more amiable man I've never met. He was engaged mainly in divorce work and I think I'm right in saying that he came to us because he felt his clerk at the time was not feeding him with enough cases, so it confirmed that I still had some reputation left in the Temple. He did well with us, eventually being appointed to the Bench. Langton Davies dealt with agricultural work, a specialised area with which our chambers had for many years been associated. He believed, and rightly as it turned out, that he would eventually inherit James Leonard's appointment as Junior Counsel to the Ministry of Agriculture and Fisheries.

So gradually the chambers moved into a higher key. I still kept a watchful eye on the political scene in the hope that Quintin might soon be back with us, though I knew the longer he was away the more difficult would be his chances of re-establishing himself. It was ironic to me that the historic office of First Lord, which was the reason for his leaving the Bar, was one he only held for four months. He later became in turn Minister for

145

Education, Conservative Party Chairman, Minister of Science and Lord Privy Seal, and, strangely in view of his lack of interest in organized games, Minister with responsibility for Sport.

With the passing of the Life Peerages Act in 1963, I had reason once again to furrow my brows. This could have further repercussions, for it would allow Quintin to renounce his title and, should Harold Macmillan decide to resign his premiership, with his high standing in Parliament he might well be in line as successor. I was nearer to the truth than I thought. I later learned that Quintin had been told by Macmillan that he was his favoured choice as a successor, so that when unexpectedly Mr Harold Macmillan did resign during the Conservative Conference at Blackpool, Quintin had every reason to believe that the political crown was his. That Alec Douglas Home was chosen is now history.

When I heard the full story, my feelings were mixed. I knew how great the disappointment must have been for Quintin, and I felt bitter at the scurvy way he seemed to have been treated. I also wondered whether it wouldn't have been better to have been the one-time clerk of the prime minister, than the present clerk of a should-have-been. I wondered too whether, when he came to return to the Bar, his character might have reacted to the hurt and whether any possible change might adversely affect his work. Nevertheless, I still welcomed the chance to have him back home, in chambers. In the event I need have had no misgivings. Quintin had a rare philosophy of life, which gave him a sense and direction in all he did, and supplied him with consolation in misfortune, and courage when he was tempted to despair.

Chapter Eight

It was after the narrow Conservative defeat in the general election of 1964 that Quintin returned to chambers. I use the word narrow because it only needed a quarter of a million votes to have swung to the Tories for victory to have been theirs. There was a strong conviction, and not only among his friends, that with Quintin as leader they would more than have achieved this.

Sensibly he realised that after eight years absence from the Bar his Law was rusty. He also knew that solicitors and their clients were suspicious of barristers that led double lives, and that though he had made the return once, there was a widespread feeling that he wouldn't be able to do it again. He had therefore to be capable of meeting the challenge. For my part, I had to make sure that when he was ready I had the right case to offer him; one that would give scope for oratory, provide a worthy opponent, and attract both the attention of the lawyers and the general public.

I also had an more immediate job to do; I had to resort to a public relations exercise. I wanted it voiced around that Quintin was back at the Bar, raring to go and was as good, if not better, than ever. The Temple was well situated for such a ploy, since it lies behind Fleet Street. It had to be delicately executed, first because barristers can be disciplined for seeming to advertise for work, and second because Quintin, who knew better than most politicians how to hit the limelight, shunned any publicity that affected his legal career. His taciturnity did not suit me or the occasion. I had to move carefully among the journalists who hung around the Courts, or frequented the drinking houses. There were too many who were looking for dirt about Quintin. It was strange that there were those who seemed to think there must be something discreditable about a man who had been selected as a potential leader by his fellows but had then failed to achieve power; and that they felt that any opportunity of knocking him was fair practice. Like my Sabrina, I was not one of those who thought that there was no such thing as bad publicity, so I chose my newsmen carefully. I employed the usual techniques, the 'strictly between ourselves', 'this bit is not for publication', which send journalists rushing back to their offices. It served its purpose, and I managed to get some complimentary comment in the news and gossip columns.

After a few months Quintin felt he was ready to go into court, and the moment was right. I had been offered a brief for him to lead for the defence in an action between Twentieth Century Fox Film Corporation and Anglo-American Film Productions. It concerned two film versions of the story of Antony and Cleopatra; the one made by Fox was a multi-million dollar 'masterpiece' starring Richard Burton, Elizabeth Taylor and Rex Harrison; the other, *Carry on Cleo* was a farcical piece of slapstick, featuring such comics as Sid James, Kenneth Williams, Kenneth Connor, Joan Simms, Charles Hawtrey and Amanda Barrie. There is, of course, no copyright in history. However, the 'Carry On' film producers had, it was felt by Fox, denigrated their 'masterpiece' by using posters which were a take-off of those of the original publicity, and a ban was sought prohibiting their further display. Not a matter of deep and lasting legal consequence, but with Sir Andrew Clark QC, head of the Chancery Bar, leading for the plaintiffs, and Quintin leading for the defendants, it was bound to hit the headlines, and as a launching pad for Quintin it was ideal. I remember, as we went into court, he was besieged by reporters, anxious to know how he felt about his return to the legal world. 'I'll always answer questions on politics, but as you know I never comment on the Law,' he said as he brushed them aside. I dropped behind to whisper a thing or two into the ears of a couple of my friends, before following him inside the court.

It was an occasion of delight to all, a mixture of fun and wit. The two posters were exhibited in court, the one for the 'masterpiece', designed by Howard Terpning, showing Cleopatra on a divan lying between Mark Antony and Julius Caesar, and the other showing Sid James under a divan, acting the Peeping Tom to Cleo and Antony. Considerable play was made by counsel of historical detail, and Quintin got the best laugh of the case when he pointed out that Caesar had been dead for two years when the alleged events took place, and therefore it could only be assumed that the character portrayed was in fact Caesar's ghost. It mattered little that the verdict went against us. When Quintin went over to our solicitors to express his sympathy, they would have none of it, 'Our clients are delighted. They have lost nothing. Their film has really taken off and there are queues in every cinema where it's showing. We couldn't have bought this kind of publicity. We are deeply grateful to you.' Which just goes to show to what base uses the law can be put.

By appearing in 'Cleopatra' Quintin had shown that his skill was undiminished. Each succeeding case added to his reputation, and I saw to it that he was given the royal treatment. Whenever or wherever he appeared in court, I would be there doing everything in my power to make his appearance as imposing as the judge's. My juniors and I would fuss over him, laying out his books and papers as if they were holy writ. It became a kind of ceremonial, and impressed court officials and clients alike. It was the same if he went on Circuit. I remember a case in Gloucester; I went there a day ahead to prepare the way. I entertained solicitors' clerks who might be involved in cases in London. I rang the editors of the local newspapers ostensibly to advise them that Quintin would only be prepared to answer questions of a political nature, but in fact to make sure that they knew he was coming. It worked like a charm. I was the town crier announcing that the monarch was arriving incognito. The great thing was that Quintin responded brilliantly. He rose to every occasion. It was as if he had never been away. His political disappointment had left no scar; there was only one change that I noticed. During his earlier days at Number 4, he had amused himself and us by writing occasional verses; as these were no longer forthcoming, I asked him why. 'Sydney, my muse deserted me in 1963; alas I fear it will never return.' In my experience it never has, which is a great sadness.

Our visit to Gloucester concerned a murder trial. Although I don't remember the details I am reminded that it was about this time that the death sentence was abolished. There had been a deal of talk and speculation in and around the Temple as to what the consequences were likely to be. While I don't propose to engage in the arguments, I was particularly interested because of a lifelong friendship I had had with a solicitor, Harold Norman Gedge, of the firm, Gasquet, Metcalfe & Walton, who acted as under-sheriffs to the City of London. One of the firm's duties was to provide an overseer of all executions of prisoners sentenced at the Old Bailey, and, for many years both during and after the war, Harold was the solicitor designated to do this. It was a strange macabre business; after sentence was pronounced he would have to engage the services of a hangman and a deputy hangman. He would meet them in the jail late in the afternoon the day before sentence was to be carried out. The hangmen by this time had had an opportunity of observing the prisoner while he was at exercise, so that they knew his physical characteristics. His height and weight of course had previously been given to them. Many years before, Harold told me, the hangmen had not been required to arrive until an hour or so prior to the execution, but there had been a rash of absenteeism. Most hangmen were recruited from publicans, and they would often carouse through the night and early morning, and were then incapable of properly carrying out their duties. That same afternoon Harold and the hangmen would inspect and check the equipment, which was housed next to the condemned cell. On the morning of the execution, at precisely two minutes before the appointed hour, there was a procession along the corridor to the prisoner's cell, with Harold and the prison doctor leading, and the hangmen following. As they approached the cell Harold and the doctor would turn to where the scaffold was kept, while the hangmen entered the condemned

150

cell, bound the prisoner's arms behind his back with leather straps, and placed the white cap over his head. They then joined the others, the prisoner was placed on the trap, his legs also strapped, and the trap released. These proceedings took less than two minutes. After the prison doctor had pronounced death, they went to the governer's office where he, the doctor and Harold signed the notice that the sentence had been carried out. This was then hung outside the prison gates. A strange feature of this ceremony to me was that the body of the prisoner was always left hanging for at least two hours after the execution.

Again I'm not going to comment on how a man was able to tolerate such a job. It was something that had to be done, and I must say that Harold was as nice a man and as firm a friend as any in my life. Often after a hanging he would ask me to join him for coffee; he never spoke about his experiences, this was forbidden, but I could tell by his manner and expression the way the prisoner had gone to his death. There was one particular morning during the war when I noticed that he was in a rough state. I think it was as much as he could do not to break down and tell me about it. When we'd finished our coffee I advised him not to go back to the office, but to pack it in for the day and go home. It was many years later that I got the real story. 'You remember that day when I was so cut up about the hanging I had attended, Sydney? Well I can give you the details now, since it's been published in the report by the Royal Commission on Capital Punishment. We were carrying out sentence on a German spy, and as the hangmen entered the cell, he went completely berserk, screaming and fighting. He had to be overcome and dragged to the scaffold. I'd never seen a man disintegrate like that before. It was a most terrible and degrading experience.' Eventually Harold left his firm, and joined the Reed Paper Group. I continued to see him regularly. I must say that outwardly his experiences hadn't seemed to have affected him. Only he knows what they may have done inwardly.

A case with which Quintin was concerned shortly after his return was, I think, one of his most fascinating, since it put into question the laws of defamation and the competency of the jury system. It became known as the case of 'The Three Little Pigs'. On 20 September 1962, the police were informed by a firm of auctioneers, W. S. Bagshaw & Son, of the theft of three pedigree pigs during a sale at Uttoxeter, a small market town in Staffordshire. The following day Bagshaws sent details of the theft, the markings on the pigs' ears, and a description of the suspected thief to autioneers around the Midlands. On 28 September, Associated Television gave an account of the theft in their programme 'Police File'. In the circular and the programme it was stated that the thief had given his name as Boston of Rugeley. It was of course unfortunate for both Bagshaws and ATV that there happened to be a farmer in Rugeley by the name of Albert Robert Boston, who attended many auction sales around the country. Nevertheless, they should have taken more care before issuing the circular or screening the feature. Not unnaturally, farmer Boston was put to a deal of embarrassment and ridicule from his business associates and friends, and wanted compensation through the courts. The television company did their best to make amends by twice broadcasting apologies to Mr Boston, but this did not satisfy him and eventually they settled for damages of £7,000.

So it became a straight contest between Boston and the Bagshaws. Quintin was leading for the Bagshaws, and on their behalf argued that they had not intended to refer to Mr Boston as the thief, that they had not been moved by malice and also pleaded 'qualified privilege'. What on the face of it looked a simple case dragged on for fifteen days. It was part of our strategy to raise as many questions as possible and so to confuse the jury; it was Theo Mathew over again. Theo encouraged such a situation in the expectation that the jury would answer some of them wrongly and thus thwart the result for the other side. It may sound a peculiar practice but it must be remembered that it is counsel's duty to do the best he can for his client; it is for the judge to ensure, in his summing up, that the jury can see the wood for the trees. In this case the judge clouded the issue with a summing-up of 26,000 words and finally left them thirteen questions to answer.

There had been little doubt from the beginning that the jury was on poor Mr Boston's side. They considered their verdict for over five hours. Then, as the foreman gave the answers to the questions that had been posed, it became more obvious that they intended to find in his favour. They agreed that he had been libelled, and awarded him £11,000 damages, but finally they found that the Bagshaws' motive in their action had not been instigated through malice. Quintin had not been in court for the verdict, but his junior Maurice Drake was swift to see that this was the answer we had been hoping for. He jumped to his feet and declared that if there was no malice there could be no libel. It was a terrible blow for the lawyers on the Boston side. They could see the £11,000 fluttering out of the window. The jury were stupefied by it; they obviously has no idea of the hornet's nest they had stirred up. The judge deferred his judgement until the following day when he ruled that Mr Boston's action had failed on this one point of Law. We were given judgement and costs, which meant that by exercising his legal rights Boston had lost £20,000 plus of course the £11,000 which, earlier on the day before, he thought he had been awarded.

The matter did not rest there. Mr Boston's lawyers entered a notice of appeal, asking for a fresh trial. They also interviewed members of the jury in their anxiety to make certain that this time Mr Boston would win. Now, while it is forbidden for any juryman to discuss a case with anyone outside the jury during a trial, there is no rule to stop them giving an opinion afterwards. Nevertheless, it was in my experience unprecedented, and I'm sure was not, nor would not be, encouraged by those who administer the Law. His solicitors did, however, get an affidavit from each of the twelve members of the jury, to the effect that they had meant to find that Bagshaws had been moved by malice, and that they had been misled into giving the wrong reply. There was no question of them having been cajoled into signing because the *Daily Mail* conducted an independent enquiry to discover the reasons why the jury found as they did. The answers of some of the members make interesting reading. 'I can't remember the judge saying we needed to find malice. This would have meant that we had said the police were lying.'

'I thought it would have seemed that we were saying that the police had been acting maliciously, and I thought that we can't call the police liars.'

'I was under the impression that malice and libel were two separate issues. I understand malice to be a heavy blow to a person's character.'

'One of the jury said that if we found that there had been malice we would be calling the police liars. I didn't want to cause trouble with the police.'

When the case came before the Court of Appeal, the judges refused to allow the jury's statement to be produced, one of them saying that to admit such evidence would mean the destruction of the whole system of trial by jury. The court ruled that the finding of 'no malice' was correct. Once again the wretched Mr Boston had to meet the costs, which meant that the total had risen to around £30,000. While the case ended there, the discussion didn't. There were leading articles in newspapers. Questions were asked in the House, and efforts were made to amend the defamation laws, but the Attorney General would have none of it. He said that the verdict was justified, and that members of parliament could not sit in judgement on the proceedings of the Appeal Court, and that clearly the Court of Appeal thought the verdict was the only proper result of the case and that Boston should have had no hope of winning. I think this case shows more than any other that upholding the law does not always mean that justice has been done; it hinged on the interpretation of the word malice, which has a harsher meaning outside the courts than it has inside.

There is much that could be written of Quintin's experiences at the Bar; he though is the only man to do it, and although I know he has been approached a number of times, like his father he has always refused. This I think is a pity because from the few glimpses he has given of his feelings towards the Law in his political autobiography, *The Door Wherein I Went*, such a book would be of great value to lawyers, present and future. I am only able to outline the man as I knew him, drawn as I have watched from the wings, but of the inner force that drove him to the top of his profession, yet still allowed him to give his time in great measure to politics, he alone has the answer. What has always amazed me is how a man of such intellect and ability could still retain his youthful naivety and boyish charm; how he could still thrust his fingers into his hair and make it stick up like an urchin's; how he had no regard for any kind of public image, and how he retained the ability to laugh at himself.

Although the years 1964 to 1970 were harvest years, there was all too soon the spectre of a general election and Tory victory. I was comforted in a way though by the popular success that Harold Wilson and the Labour Government appeared to be enjoying, and by Quintin's predictions that they would almost certainly be returned again.

I was able to be of some assistance to Mr Harold Wilson before the dreaded election. I was sitting in my room one Friday morning in July, musing over the fortnight's holiday on the Costa del Sol that lay ahead for Do and me. We were booked to fly to Spain that night and I looked forward to days in the sun, and nights we would dance away. The phone rang, and was answered by one of the secretaries. Suddenly I became conscious that her conversation seemed strange for a barrister's office, 'Go on, pull the other one, you'll be asking us to act for Doctor Crippen next.' I made gestures indicating that I wanted to know what was going on. She put her hand over the mouth piece, 'It's some joker who says he wants Mr Hogg to represent Harold Wilson in an action with a pop group called The Move. It's all right, I can cope with him.' 'What did he say his name was?' 'Some good man called Derek,' she replied. I quickly took the phone from her. It was a call from the Chief Clerk of a leading firm of London solicitors, Goodman, Derek & Company, and the secretary had indeed heard the message correctly; Quintin was required to act for the prime minister, and it did concern the pop group. My immediate job was to get Quintin to a conference by eleven o'clock, otherwise the solicitors would have to go else-where. Knowing that Quintin would enjoy the quixotic situation, I gave my promise. It proved difficult to keep as we had no idea where he was. Eventually we tracked him down at his barber's, and he arrived at the meeting with only seconds to spare. The case concerned the publication of an obscene caricature of Harold Wilson, which the group were proposing to use to publicise a record. The prime minister and his legal advisers thought it necessary to stop the circulation of such defamatory material, and wanted it done fast. After the conference was over Quintin returned to chambers and asked me to find a judge who was willing to hear our application for emergency relief. By now it was well into Friday afternoon, not a time when judges were easily available or anxious to engage in any further work, so my task wasn't easy. I could see our holiday in Spain becoming more and more remote and began to wish that I had not been so eager to snatch the phone from the secretary. Eventually however Mr Justice O'Connor agreed to an emergency hearing, and we were able to stop the publication and distribution of the offending material. What interested me about this case was why Mr Wilson had engaged Quintin. The answer was simple; he went to his close friend Lord Goodman who headed the firm of Goodman, Derek & Company, who asked whether Mr Harold Wilson had any preference for whom he wanted to act for him. 'The best man for the job,' was the brief reply. 'That man happens to be Hogg, a political opponent.' 'Then get him,' said Wilson. I couldn't help reflecting that it was a pity Barbara Castle hadn't followed the example of her leader.

As the general election of 1970 approached, I tried to take stock of my situation. I was now sixty-nine, rising seventy. I'd served in the Temple for fifty-five years. I was not a poor man. Even without a pension Do and I would be comfortably off should I decide to retire; but I didn't want to, most certainly not if Labour remained in power. If the Tories won, and Quintin was given some high office as was probable, then matters would be different. But how different? In any case would my life have any real purpose? My daughter had now married, and was living in Australia. Do seemed to enjoy pottering around our mews house in Kensington, and she had many friends and acquaintances; would she want me idling around the place and interfering with her social life? I was still mentally alert, and I enjoyed working. I

156

knew no other life. Was it worth giving it all up? Yet what was the alternative – to continue like some old soldier and eventually just fade away? I pondered over these questions daily without coming to any decision.

Then one day Quintin called me into his room. 'Sydney, I've been thinking about the future.' 'So have I,' I replied. 'Well, before you come to any decisions, I'd like you to consider what I have to suggest. It looks very much to me as if a Labour government will be returned again, and the opinion polls seem to agree with me. If they do it will mean that I shall continue at the Bar. Now neither of us is getting any younger, and I think we deserve to take life a little easier. If you agree, I would like you to remain in chambers as my clerk, looking only after me. We can choose the kind of work we want to do, and at the same time take a rest or a holiday when we want one. We can engage another clerk to take over the work of the other barristers in chambers. What do you say to that?' It seemed the ideal way out of my dilemma. I agreed straight away. 'That's settled then,' said Quintin. It was settled inasmuch that I gave up contemplating my future. Nevertheless, as election day drew nearer I began getting butter-flies in the stomach. On the evening of polling day, as Quintin and I parted on the steps of Number 4, he called after me, 'I'll bet you're praying for a Labour victory, aren't you Sydney?' 'Not half,' I threw back at him. He went away chuckling to himself, but I was not joking.

I sat in front of the television set until the early hours of the morning, by which time it became obvious that both the pollsters and Quintin had been wrong. By the following afternoon it was certain that Mr Heath and the Conservatives had a small, but workable, majority. I now felt I'd only one hope left, that Quintin would not be asked to take any high office, and that as an ordinary MP would at times be able to continue in practice. Two or three days passed as Mr Heath formed his Cabinet, and still Quintin had received no summons. He had, I know, expected to be appointed Home Secretary, but that job had been given to Mr Maudling. Strangely I began to feel resentful, almost personally insulted that Quintin was being passed over. Then came the crunch, he received a message to present himself at Number 10 Downing Street, and returned with the news that he had been offered the Lord Chancellorship. Never have I received news with such mixed feelings. My first reaction was one of pride. I recalled the sneering remarks of one or two of my cronies when Quintin had returned to the Bar in 1964. 'I suppose now you've got your hero back, you're going to try and make him into a future Lord Chancellor,' and I remembered my reply, 'What good is a bloody Lord Chancellor to me?' Meaning of course that I would lose a source of income forever, for once elected to the Woolsack, there could be no return for him to the Bar. Now however, money and the state of the chambers were forgotten. A barrister who had started work as a pupil in my chambers, and whom I had mothered through much of his career, had achieved the highest legal office in the land. Quintin would be head of the judiciary, a senior member of the Cabinet, the principal legal spokesman for the government, and Speaker of the House of Lords. He would also become a Life Peer. There was of course the other side of the coin. He would be lost to me forever and our plans, on which I had based my future, were now in the melting pot. 'I don't suppose you're too pleased, Sydney,' Quintin said when he told me the news. 'Well Sir, I must congratulate you,' I replied, 'and I'm very glad for Mrs Hogg's sake, now she'll be a Lady again.' This sent him off into peals of laughter, so what was for me a moving and difficult moment was easily resolved. Then, as I left his room, he gave me what I believe was his last instruction, 'Sydney, for heaven's sake remember to off-load that Lords' brief on to someone else.'

So my future plans were now in ashes. With hindsight, perhaps I should have left chambers with Quintin, but I still had Maurice Drake and Langton Davies to consider. Maurice, who had taken Silk in 1968, would become head of chambers, and both had useful practices so I decided to stay. But the old order had changed without me realising it. I had been largely preoccupied looking after Quintin, and since he was who he was, as well as head of chambers, there had been nobody to say me nay. With him gone I was expected, and rightly so, to conform to the new order of things. Numbers too had got out of hand, or so I thought; there were now twelve other young barristers in chambers, all wanting attention, and without wishing to denigrate them in any way they were not what I was used to. I now understood what was meant by the generation gap; I was not able to get through to them, and they, I'm sure, felt the same about me. Again I write this with hindsight. They were always polite and patient, and generally we rubbed along together well enough, but they were ambitious and expected to succeed at a faster pace than their predecessors. They had good reason. Legal Aid had transformed the economics of the profession. From the beginning a qualified barrister could expect to earn a reasonable living. It had also brought great changes. It meant that only the really poor could engage in private litigation. This had strengthened the position of the poor man at the expense of the person whose income was only slightly greater, and so it meant that in many instances justice was not done, and was not even seen to be done. There was also the anomaly that companies and corporations could often afford litigation, since they could claim their costs against income tax, whereas the private citizen had no such privileges. Accompanying Legal Aid was the rise in the crime rate, and in the number of petitions for divorce. The traditional type of work of our chambers had also changed, and the speed with which it was disposed of was faster; cases merely became book entries. So many of the old subtleties used by a chief clerk were no longer required. The young preferred to go it alone. A barrister's was no longer a hereditary profession where son almost automatically followed father, which meant that the traditions of the Bar, which had been passed down through the family, were now being challenged and often discarded. And everything was too big. My 'mistress' had grown obese and was wearing ill-fitting clothes. There were too many new laws, too many lawyers, too many courts and judges. I felt with Quintin, when he had said that barristers should be few, of unblemished character and highly qualified. The fact that this could no longer be said gave some force to the solicitors who wanted to break down the distinction between themselves and barristers, for no longer did another of Quintin's statements obtain: 'The solicitor is a man of business, a barrister an artist and a scholar.'

But these opinions were probably just the vapourisings of an old man, railing like so many others against youth and change. Nor was my mind filled with these thoughts during those last three years in chambers. I had an eye on a Diamond Jubilee in the Temple, something that no other clerk to my knowledge had achieved. Then came murmurs about the introduction of a new tax, Value Added Tax, and, as I was too old a dog to learn new tricks, I put my sights down and decided to retire when it was introduced.

Fate however, took a hand. Do, my wife, who had never before had a serious illness, suffered a cerebral haemorrhage, which left her completely paralysed. She was rushed to hospital and was not expected to live. Gradually she fought back, but it was a long and hard struggle. She was in hospital for many months; I was able to visit her regularly but only for short periods. Strangely, it was now more than ever that I was grateful to the Temple; to my friends of course in chambers and around, for their sympathy, understanding and kindness, but even more to my work which gave me shelter from the sadness of seeing Do, who literally and in every other way had danced through life with me, become a shadow of the woman I had known. She battled against her affliction with such courage, but watching her in those early days was self-wounding; I wanted so much to reinforce her efforts yet felt I was helpless to do anything. Later of course, when she left hospital there was so much that I could do, and I'm happy to say that our battle has been won, and although Do is not able to enjoy life as fully as she might wish her cure has been little short of miraculous.

I knew now that I must make plans for my retirement so that I could be at home to welcome Do. When I announced that I would be leaving in July 1973, I flatter myself that it caused something of a sensation; indeed those few whom I had previously thought might be glad to see the back of me appeared the most sincere in their regrets. I think it was as if everyone had considered me as a pillar of the Temple. For a time I basked in their esteem.

Yet as the days passed and the time for me to go drew nearer, I felt that after fifty-eight years service I would be leaving more with a whimper than a bang. Then the news of the farewell dinner filtered through to me, and as I began to realise its proportions I knew that I would be going with the band playing, flags flying and my head high, and that with such a send-off I would be able to forget the misgivings of the last three years and live with the memories of a life that had given such great rewards; and for better or for worse it is on memories which old men feed in the days that are left to them.